THE
ICE CREAM LOVER'S
COMPANION

I think YOU'RE the "CREAM OF THE CROP"!

THE
ICE CREAM LOVER'S
COMPANION

● ● ● ● ● ● ● ● ● ● ● ● ● ● ●

THE ULTIMATE CONNOISSEUR'S GUIDE TO
BUYING, MAKING, AND ENJOYING
ICE CREAM AND FROZEN YOGURT

Diana Rosen

CITADEL PRESS
KENSINGTON PUBLISHING CORP.
www.kensingtonbooks.com

CITADEL PRESS books are published by

Kensington Publishing Corp.
850 Third Avenue
New York, NY 10022

All Kensington titles, imprints, and distributed lines are available at special quantity discounts for bulk purchases for sales promotions, premiums, fund raising, educational, or institutional use. Special book excerpts or customized printings can also be created to fit specific needs. For details, write or phone the office of the Kensington special sales manager: Kensington Publishing Corp., 850 Third Avenue, New York, NY 10022, attn: Special Sales Department, phone 1-800-221-2647.

Kensington and the K logo Reg. U.S. Pat. & TM Office
Citadel Press is a trademark of Kensington Publishing Corp.

First printing October 2000

10 9 8 7 6 5 4 3 2 1

Printed in the United States of America

Library of Congress Cataloging-in-Publication Data

Rosen, Diana.
    The ice cream lover's companion : the ultimate connoisseur's guide to buying, making, and enjoying ice cream and frozen yogurt / Diana Rosen.
        p.   cm.
    "A Birch Lane Press book."
    Includes index.
    ISBN 1-55972-468-4
    1. Ice cream, ices, etc.   2. Frozen yogurt.   I. Title.
    TX795.R62   1998
    641.8′62—dc21   98-7556
                                                                                CIP

For my mother
Mae Z. Rosen
in remembrance of the sweet days

CONTENTS

· · · · · · · · · · · · · · · ·

Acknowledgments   9
Introduction   11
Timeline   15

THE HISTORY OF ICE CREAM   23

COLLECTING ICE CREAM MEMORABILIA   53

ICE CREAM FACTS AND TRIVIA TO FASCINATE YOUR FRIENDS   61

THE FUTURE OF ICE CREAM AND FROZEN DESSERTS   67

MAKING ICE CREAM AT HOME   71

RECIPES   85

Glossary   147
Bibliography   154
Index   155

REMEMBER Miss Muffett,
who sat on a tuffet,

While eating her curds and
whey?

Now when you spy her, you'll
see she has by her,

A dish of Ice Cream every day.

Acknowledgments

So many generous people in the ice cream and dairy industries helped in my research of America's favorite dessert. Thanks, in no particular order, to Howard Waxman, editor, *Ice Cream Reporter;* Amy S. Kemp, associate technical editor, *Journal of Dairy Science;* Norman F. Olson, professor emeritus, department of Food Science, University of Wisconsin; the staff of the International Dairy Association; Jennifer Korolishin, communications manager, International Ice Cream Association; Ed Marks, presenter of the Successful Ice Cream Retailing Seminar and guest lecturer for the Penn State Ice Cream Short Course sponsored by the Penn State College of Agricultural Sciences; Diane Lueders, owner of Coleman's Ice Cream, Lancaster, Pennsylvania, and 1998 president of the National Association of Ice Cream and Frozen Yogurt Retailers; Thomas Palchak, manager, University Creamery, Penn State College of Agricultural Sciences; Diane McIntyre, public relations director, Dreyer's Ice Cream; Terry Murphy, director of corporate communications, Baskin-Robbins; Dean Peters, director of communications, International Dairy Queen, Inc.; Ron Hingst of PR Services, Inc., for A&W Root Beer; Michelle Watson, IDFA (International Dairy Foods Association); Will Conyngham and Frank Conyngham, Hillside Farms; Turkey Hill Farms; Marble Slab Creamery.

For the delightful ice cream paper ephemera, thank you, Richard Warren.

Thank you American composer Meyer Kupferman, Atril Cinco Ensemble Mexicano Contemporaneo, and its conductor Roberto Limon.

Thank you to the many people outside the dairy industry who helped with questions related to history, nonmilk products, and all the other miscellany that went into the research of this book: Jane Zukin, author of *Raising Your Child Without Milk* and *Dairy-*

Free Cookbook and editor, "The Newsletter for People With Lactose Intolerance and Milk Allergy"; The Marin City Library, the Sausalito Library, and the San Francisco Library and their staffs who were infinitely patient as I searched the stacks; the Internet, and related sources; the Library of Congress, the libraries of Mount Vernon and Montebello, and the British Library and Frances Woods, curator, Oriental and Indian Affairs Collection, and author of *Did Marco Polo Go to China?*

Thanks to chefs extraordinaire Robert Wemischner, Terri Hayward of the Perfect Purée of Napa Valley, Cathy Brown, Mara Teitel, and Carolyn Manzi.

For their trips down memory lane for Ice Cream Moments, I thank Ronald and Phyllis Anatole, Steve B., William J. Birnes, Sally Champe, Ms. Dona, Kate Grant, Marie Henry, G. Simpson, and Robert Wemischner.

Thanks to Carol Publishing Group and Birch Lane Press, and to my editor, Monica Harris.

Thank you to Dr. Dan the Computer Man, Gabriele Meiringer, and staff of Writers' Computer Store of Sausalito; Devan Shah of India Tea Importers, and "kulfi expert"; and my ever-supportive friends: Karen Benke, Suzanne J. Brown, William E. Johnston Jr., The Merlin Family, Diana Bouchard Payette, Karen Strange, and Amy Ulmer for the encouraging words.

INTRODUCTION

....

My tongue is smiling.
—Abigail Trillin, age four, after eating chocolate ice cream.
(from *Alice, Let's Eat* by Calvin Trillin)

Ice cream always reminds me of my idyllic childhood summers: days spent at the community swimming pool cannonballing into the middle of the chlorine-scented blue water; evenings carrying just-washed mayonnaise jars on twilight journeys to catch fireflies; nights spent toasting marshmallows over campfires until they were burnt on the outside and gooey on the inside, then laid atop chocolate bars with graham crackers to make that oddly named treat every camper or scout learned to make, s'mores.

In those innocent days, we welcomed carnivals traveling the summer circuit to our small town, with their cacophony of barkers shouting over the pipe organ music of the merry-go-round, punctuated by the squeals from passengers on the Ferris wheel as our family walked down the straw-covered ground, enveloped by the smells of constantly heated popcorn and the sticky sweetness of cotton candy on a stick.

No summer memory of mine, however, is as gentle or as welcoming as the tinkle-tinkle of the big white ice cream van chugging up Delaware Avenue at dusk, the signal for my friends and me to put down our jump ropes, stuff shiny jacks and small red rubber balls into our pockets, lay down the other toys of summer, and run to the waiting truck where we made our choices of Fudgsicles, Drumsticks, Creamsicles, or ice cream sandwiches. Unwrapping the sticky papers, we would sit on the curb, and fall into silence as we ate our treats slowly, doing our best to make them last longer, for soon it would be time to head into the house for the close of another precious summer vacation day.

Other summer ice cream memories surface, especially of Page Dyer setting up his wooden-barreled hand-crank ice cream maker that he'd fill up with fresh, sweet, juicy peaches floating in heavy milk. Like magic, all of us neighborhood kids assembled in his backyard to form a line, waiting excitedly for the thrill of a turn cranking the machine (not realizing what a Tom Sawyer gesture it was on Mr. Dyer's part).

Of course, his own seven children would have been enough to make the mixture into velvety ice cream, but it wouldn't have been the same adventure for us. No peach ice cream ever tasted as good as Mr. Dyer's. I still don't know if it was the freshness of the peaches, the pureness of the milk, or just cranking that metal hanger till my shoulder hurt that was the perfect ingredient for this ultimate summer pleasure.

In the simpler times in which I grew up, going to Hagan's Ice Cream Parlor was a special treat. There at the soda fountain, piled as high as the eye of a child sitting on the red-vinyl and polished-chrome stool, were magnificent sculptures to be eaten with icy spoons. Sundaes of indescribable construction fascinated us all—pure vanilla ice cream, sometimes topped with thickly sweet butterscotch syrup or, more often, topped with rich, velvety dark chocolate, chopped peanuts, and the perfunctory maraschino cherry.

Sometimes we sipped the yin-yang of ice cream sodas, the sweet smoothness of ice cream brought to a frothy confection with the tart soda, served with that most delightful invention, a paper straw, complete with paper sheath that one could, with unbridled joy, blow into the face of an unsuspecting sibling. Other times, the choice would be to watch the sage green, art-deco-style machine rev its magic in the stainless steel cup: whipping up a chocolate malt or milkshake, its icy chill biting the palate, cooling us down to our toes.

In those days before air conditioning was common or the highways bulged with traffic, a summer night's drive was a carefree way to cool off from the Pennsylvania heat and humidity. No drive would be complete without a stop at the Dairy Queen, home of my mother's favorite dessert. It was a peculiarly comforting treat, softer, creamier, less biting cold than store-bought ice cream.

The waffle-patterned sugar cones, gripped in the hands of both parents and children, were like miniature torches with white waves of ice cream instead of fire, a visual pun on Old Liberty, except we shouted, "Give me your hot and cranky, your people yearning for something cool and sweet. . . ."

One of the most endearing and reassuring things to know about these memories is that they can be yours today. True, the Dairy Queens, Foster Freezes, and A&W Root Beer Stands are located primarily on offshoots of old Route 66 and in smaller towns, but they're still here. Some have married other companies to offer a full menu of foods from hamburgers and fries to the same steady diet of frosty shakes and soft ice cream cones.

The 7–11, which replaced the tiny neighborhood grocer, carries Drumsticks, ice cream sandwiches, and Creamsicles in its floor freezers, and you can sometimes get sundaes, sodas, and milkshakes at coffee shops, the remaining soda fountains, fifties revivalist diners like Johnny Rockets or Ed Debevic's, and even some delicatessens.

Ice cream memories like these say "America" to me, although I know that ice cream was not invented here. So many spins on this centuries-old dessert have been created in the United States, from Eskimo Pies to ice cream cakes, that it's hard not to think of ice cream as an intrinsically American dessert.

Ice creams have improved enormously, and the boutique brands are offering taste combinations that are intriguing and quality ingredients that are simply superb. As always, your local ice cream maker surely has the freshest, most flavorful ice cream. Umquardt in Oregon, Coleman's in Pennsylvania, Bud's of San Francisco, Greenfield's in Atlanta, or Blue Bell and Edy's throughout the South taste particularly good because they haven't traveled three thousand miles to reach you.

Marble Slab and Swensen's stores, which create their own ice creams on-site, are significantly more flavorful; it's hard to beat freshness that takes only the time needed to go from the back of the store kitchen to the front of the store counter.

Ben & Jerry's, Dove Bars, Double Rainbow, Steve's, Portofino, and many other manufacturers are following the leadership of Häagen-Dazs in the role of superb store-bought ice creams.

What all these new players in the field of frozen desserts are doing is going backward, by using prime, pure ingredients, while going forward, with more sophisticated flavors and combinations. To these and those to come, we say hooray!

Today, with the yuppification of nearly every foodstuff, ice cream is now available in flavors once thought of as exotic. Moreover, anyone requiring low-fat foods need not sacrifice frozen delectables for desserts. Sorbets have acquired a purer fruit flavor, as evidenced from Dole fruit sherbets on a stick to Edy's Whole Fruit in the pint. Häagen-Dazs has scored with its chocolate sherbet on a stick, and the fruit sorbets of Double Rainbow are heart-stopping good.

In this book, we'll take a glimpse at the history of this hugely popular dessert, weaving in some of the many sayings, comments, songs, and poems it has inspired to demonstrate how ice cream has seeped into both our art and culture.

Our recipes capture both the experimental and the ultra-conservative. Yes, we include vanilla and chocolate, still the two top-sellers most everywhere. The tools to make sorbets and granitas are already in your kitchen; and although the latest electric ice cream makers are engineering marvels, we have to admit that the old hand-cranking freezer is still worth the additional effort for the most superb ice cream.

Whatever your passion, you can make frozen desserts at home that are tasty, incredibly fresh, and healthful. Fresh ice creams can be made without salt; ices and granitas are made without milk or cream for low-cholesterol treats; and rice milk, soy milk, and tofu are good substitutes for the lactose-intolerant and the stringent vegetarian.

The Ice Cream Lover's Companion is a book about the pleasures of this ancient treat and its many variations. We offer it to you with the reminder that "life is short, eat dessert first." Make it ice cream.

Diana Rosen

TiMELiNE
. . . .

1560s Blasius Villafranca, a physician from Spain, invents the first home ice cream freezer.

1569 Battista della Porta writes in his "Magnus Naturalis" that various salts added to snow could produce very low temperatures, thus penning the first words about artificial ice.

1670 Café Procope is established as a place to buy exquisite coffees, chocolates, and the newest sensation from Italy, *eaux d'Italie,* or ices as they are now called. Becomes one of 250 ice cream merchants in seventeenth-century Paris. The café, splendidly ornate, still exists.

1744 Ice cream is first mentioned in American letters when William Black, a guest of Governor Thomas Bladen of Maryland, writes in his journal of having strawberry ice cream during dinner at the governor's mansion. Prior to this letter, most references to this dessert were as a milk ice, cream ice, or butter ice, reflecting the ingredients used.

1768 *L'Art de Bien Faire des Glaces D'Office; ou Les Vrais Principes,* the first book devoted exclusively to ice cream recipes, is published.

1776 The first U.S. ice cream parlor opens up in New York City.

1794 The first book of sorbet recipes, written by Dr. Filippo Baldini and called *De'Sorbetti Saggio,* is published in Naples.

1830 The soda fountain begins its long reign as an American icon. What first began as an alternative to the bar evolved into a family center where pharmacists doled out sodas for health. From there, an entire American culture was born as each confection was created: ice cream sundaes, ice cream sodas, banana splits, and more.

1847   Patrons of Andrew's Eagle Ice Cream Saloon in Pittsburgh get more than a dish of ice cream for their quarter tab on September 11. That Saturday night was the first public performance of Stephen Foster's song "Oh! Susanna." Some music historians cite that date as the birth of modern American popular music.

1891   Escoffier creates *Les Peches au Cygne*, "peaches of the swan," for Australian opera singer Nellie Melba, who dined at his restaurant in London's Savoy Hotel. Altering the recipe later in 1899, Escoffier added a raspberry sauce to his vanilla ice cream and peach dessert and served it as the grand finale at the opening of the Carlton Hotel. One of the guests was Miss Melba, and in her honor it has been known as Peaches Melba ever since.

1896   Italo Marchiony invents a cuplike holder for selling ice cream. Patented in 1903, it was a metal cup with small handles that he used in his popular ice cream carts on the streets of New York.

1904   The World Exposition is held in St. Louis, with more than fifty ice cream vendors. Here, the ice cream cone was "invented" and set off a highly contested debate, still raging today.

1906   President Theodore Roosevelt signs the first Food and Drug Act, regulating the manufacture of ice cream and other foods. Want to know more? Check out the U.S. Government Printing Office for the Code of Federal Regulations, Title 21, Part 135. Ironically (or purposely?), these are updated every April 1.

1921   Christian Nelson of Iowa, in partnership with Russell Stover of candy fame, creates the chocolate-covered ice cream bar and calls it the Eskimo Pie. The patent, alas, was deemed invalid in 1928, although the original company still exists.

1923   Candyman Harry Burt Sr. of Ohio creates the Good Humor sucker and Frank Epperson of California invents the Popsicle, which he originally called the Epsicle. (Following in the eponymous shoes of Epperson, H. P. Hood of Boston made a tub-shaped paper cup he called the Hoodsie, which in 1924 was renamed the Dixie cup.)

1924   Roy Allen registers the name A&W Root Beer and the A&W logo five years after starting his first hamburger and root beer stand in Lodi, California, on June 20, 1919. (**A** was for Allen and **W** was for Wright, named for his partner, Frank Wright.)

His root beer, from a recipe purchased from an Arizona pharmacist, sold for five cents a mug. Allen retired in 1950 after developing A&W Restaurants, Inc., into America's original fast food chain. The company has undergone changes and expansions under several owners and is now operated by a group of investors headed by Sid Feltenstein, who bought it from Cadbury Schweppes in 1994.

1926   Clarence Vogt of Kentucky invents the first successful continuous freezer, enabling ice cream makers to mass produce their product when previously they had been able to make only one batch at a time.

1928   Joseph Edy and William Dreyer begin what is called Grand Ice Cream on Grand Avenue in Oakland, California. Edy brought confectionery and retail experience and Dreyer brought experience in the ice cream industry. They created Rocky Road, Toasted Almond, and Candy Mint flavors. Today the company, now known as Dreyer's Grand Ice Cream, has several product lines: Dreyer's, Edy's Grand Ice Cream, Edy's Whole Fruit Sorbet (aka Dreyer's Whole Fruit Sorbets), and Portofino's. In a joint venture agreement, it produces Starbucks coffee ice creams made with premium coffee extracts. It also serves as a jobbing manufacturer for Healthy Choice ice creams.

The company's famous "Old No. 1" delivery truck, a classic 1920 Model T Ford half-ton truck, still sports its original four-cylinder, twenty-horsepower engine and cruises at thirty miles per hour, although it's been known to max out at fifty miles per hour. The antique truck is no longer used for deliveries but for special events throughout the country such as ice cream socials, auto shows, and parades. The truck held metal containers in one- to five-gallon sizes, which were placed into a larger wooden tub with ice and salt tamped down around the metal cans to keep the ice cream frozen for the several hours delivery would take. Austin Archer delivered ice cream in the San Francisco area for many years and drove one of the two original delivery routes. His son Ed Archer is the current caretaker of the truck.

1929   Edy and Dreyer add nuts and marshmallows to their ice cream mix, cutting marshmallows up with their wives' sewing scissors to make bite-size pieces. (They also developed "toasted almonds" to keep them from getting soggy in ice cream and added peppermint as a flavor.) The company is credited with putting chocolate chip cookie dough into a vanilla ice cream mixture in 1991; earlier, in 1983, it added an Oreo-cookie flavor.

1930   I. C. Parker, advertising manager for Pangburn Candy and Ice Cream Co. in Texas, creates the Drumstick, a chocolate nut sundae in a sugar cone. He went on to form a company for his new product, the Frozen Drumstick Company.

1938   J. F. "Grandpa" McCullough and son Alex debut their "soft serve" ice cream, made at a lower temperature, on August 4 at Sherb's Ice Cream Shop in Kankahee, Illinois.

1939   Harry Oltz signs an agreement to extend the manufacturing rights of his soft-serve freezer, patented on May 18, 1937, to J. F. McCullough for Illinois, Wisconsin, and the states west of the Mississippi River, enabling the McCulloughs to launch Dairy Queen.

1939   Tom Carvel invents his own freezer, enabling him to make an ice cream that is softer and less icy than traditional hard ice cream and setting off an explosion of soft ice cream imitators of his Carvel Company.

1940   The first Dairy Queen store, owned by Sherb Noble and managed by Jim and Grace Elliott, opens June 22, 1940, in Joliet, Illinois. Noble went on to own many Dairy Queens and was associated with the company for more than fifty-two years.

1945   Irv Robbins opens an ice cream store in Glendale, California, called Snowbird, featuring twenty-one flavors. The following year, he teamed up with his competitor and brother-in-law, Burt Baskin, to form Baskin-Robbins.

1948   In answer to requests by Dairy Queen to help speed production, Joseph Shapiro of Maryland Cup Corporation creates the first flat-bottom cone. His company was later renamed Sweetheart Cup.

1970s   Frozen yogurt is introduced in the United States, most likely by food giants Dannon and Beatrice in 1972. It was an immediate dud because the tang of the yogurt culture was unfamiliar to most American palates.

1977   Dreyer's Grand Ice is sold to T. Gary Rogers and William F. Cronk III for $1 million. Currently it has more than eighteen hundred employees nationwide, with five manufacturing facilities in Texas, California, and Indiana. Its official taster, John Harrison, has had his taste buds insured for a cool million dollars. Dreyer's/Edy's currently has nearly 13 percent of the U.S. ice cream market, over five hundred other competitors. Blue Bell of Texas is Number Two. Gross sales for each company top $800 million.

1980   Edy's introduces the first commercial frozen yogurt nationally that is instantly popular because of its sweeter, less tangy taste, following the national edict to make a confection out of everything.

1982   The Ice Screamers, an association of collectors of ice cream memorabilia, is founded by Ed Marks. The annual convention, now held in Lancaster, Pennsylvania, every June, draws hundreds of people to display and view scoops, freezers, paper ephemera, and other collectibles.

1982   July is proclaimed National Ice Cream Month, designating the third Sunday as National Ice Cream Day, following more than four decades of lobbying by the ice cream industry. It's now your patriotic duty to eat ice cream the third Sunday of every July.

1985   Dairy Queen launches a new product, the Blizzard, an upside-down milk shake eaten with a "spork." The product, a mixture of its classic vanilla and a wide selection of flavors, was its most successful, selling 100 million in its first year. It remains the company's biggest selling treat.

The
Ice Cream Lover's
Companion

The History of Ice Cream

It looks so grassy but still has a crisp texture,
It appears congealed and yet it seems to float,
Like jade, it breaks at the bottom of the dish;
As with snow, it melts in the light of the sun.
—Yang Wanli, 1127–1206, a Sung poet

Legends abound about the origin of ice cream, and most, alas, are apocryphal. What we do know is that fruit- or wine-flavored "ices" were common among such diverse peoples as the Arabs, Persians, Romans, and Chinese thousands of years ago. These ices were simple pleasures before the concepts of marketing, distribution, and shelf life became part of the general lexicon of foodstuffs.

It's been difficult for historians to pinpoint an exact time of invention, but we know that early in the fourth century Romans enjoyed ices, and, at least four thousand years ago the Chinese, who already knew how to harvest ice, mixed ices with fruit and wine. Generally, all these "ices" were like our present-day slushes, more drink than food.

The lone exception to these water ices was *kumiss*, a beverage of fermented mare's milk common in Mongolia and nearby parts of Russia. A Chinese dish made from fermented goat's milk and rice was mentioned as a casual reference in some books but since milk is so uncommon in the Chinese diet, we can only view this example as legend, too.

THAT WILD AND CRAZY MARCO

For nearly seven centuries, romance has surrounded the Italian explorer Marco Polo, who is credited with bringing ice cream from China to Italy. Although there is no doubt that the man traveled extensively for more than two decades during the twelfth century, much of his reportage seems to have been more self-promotion than reality.

Whether Polo ever tasted ice *cream* is the point of contention. He certainly never tasted it in China, if he went there at all. German Mongolist Herbert Franke certainly gave Polo many benefits of the doubt, but even he believed Polo got many of his ideas of China not from direct travel but from Arab and Persian sources. This is substantiated by many accounts because Polo was well known for his ability to mix up geography.

While Polo mentions Kublai Khan, nothing in Chinese references of that age mentions Polo, or any Italians. Despite references by Western observers who visited China before his own alleged travels, Polo does not comment on such phenomena as the Great Wall, women with bound feet, and tea drinking. (If he had, Italy would be drinking chai instead of espresso.) In her book *Did Marco Polo Go to China?* Frances Woods finds these omissions of twelfth-century Chinese life striking. As curator of the Oriental and Indian Affairs Collection in the British Library, Woods believes Polo probably never got farther than Persia (now Iran), thus busting the myth that he ever explored China.

As for Polo's Chinese observations, he probably obtained them by less than noble ways. According to modern historians, he spent more time in jail than traveling, but he used that time well, listening to his cellmates share many a tale of their own explorations, which Polo carefully recorded. It is most likely that Rusticello of Pisa, a well-known mercenary of the time and, fittingly, a writer of popular romance, met Polo in prison in Genoa in 1299, following a sea battle in which he was taken prisoner. Together, they collaborated on Polo's seminal book, *Descriptions of the World (Divisaent dou Monde)*, the source of his reputation and a book that for more than five centuries made a tremendous impact on world history, geography, and mythology. Perhaps if Christopher Columbus had not used it as a guide, he would have known he was not heading toward Asia.

Woods also says that Polo probably never traveled farther than his family's trading posts on the Black Sea and in Constantinople, arguing that travelers attempting to trace his footsteps always seem to get lost at this point. She also believes that Polo may have borrowed details of China travel from Arabic or Persian guidebooks that match those used by famous Arab and Persian writers of the day.

This is not to say that Polo never ate "ices," which were common throughout the Middle East, particularly in Persia and the nearby Arab countries where he, his father, and his uncle traveled for some twenty-four years. The Arabs had many forms of ices for drinks and foods and were early pioneers in developing ice, as were indeed the Chinese. (They also had a form of that other famous foodstuff that Polo allegedly brought back from China to Italy: spaghetti. The Arabs called it *itriya*, and it was certainly a common item during the time the Polos traveled.)

We do know that neither the Chinese nor the Arabs had desserts made with milk, which of course is the primary ingredient in what we now call ice cream.

CHINESE WERE FIRST (WE THINK)

"Harvesting" ice was done by putting salt onto cool water. It was such a demanding and full-time job that King Tang of the Shang Dynasty (1122–480 B.C.) employed ninety-four ice men, among his more than 2,200 servants.

The job of the ice men was arduous and back-breaking. The ice men first had to harvest the ice by cutting huge chunks in uniform shapes, load it onto rough-hewn carts and, using sturdy horses, transport these carts full of heavy ice to stone icehouses, built by hand. The ice stayed in the stone buildings where they helped keep foods preserved and fresh for the king and his court, often for many months at a time.

During the summer, the ice was also used in fruit and wine slushes or iced desserts, similar to what we now call water ices. Such ices were eaten in the era of the Northern Song Dynasty (A.D. 960 to 1127) and during the fourteenth-century reign of the Mogul Court (A.D. 1526–1761).

The first reference in Chinese history to any milk product, cool or iced, is a fermented milk made during the T'ang Dynasty (A.D. 618–907). Milk from the water buffalo, goat, or cow was mixed with camphor, allowed to ferment, and then cooled. I shudder to think how the camphor affected the milk, but suspect it added a distinctive, shall we say, "tang."

Another reference to milk our research of Chinese cuisine uncovered is a mixture of rice and milk frozen to create a tangy milk dish; this actually might be the true origin of "frozen yogurt." Many Caucasians were known for drinking or eating fermented milk products, so it might be surmised that some of these people traveled to Mongolia then on to China, or vice versa, and incorporated fermented milk products into their diets.

The Mongols and the northern Russians still drink a fermented milk product similar to kumiss, described on page 23. It is made with mare's milk and fermented into a beverage that has been described as refreshing and sparkling, and that is usually served in a teacup-size container called a *piala*. This drink first appeared during the Yuan Mongol Era (A.D. 1279–1368).

Other than those just noted, the Chinese have no recipes using milk or milk products in their enormously sophisticated cuisine, and ice cream is not made in China today except by foreign restaurants.

ALEXANDER AND NERO WERE NOT BEN & JERRY

In ancient Greece and Rome, as in China, ices were popular as a cool way to deal with the scorching summers.

Alexander the Great's love for iced beverages during the fourth century B.C. was no doubt dependent upon his unending supply of Roman slaves. These strong, young men ran in relays up and down the Alps, carrying loads of snow down to the palace. There, the snow was mixed with either wine or fruit to help Al slake his royal thirst. Of course, his staff had to anticipate when he would be thirsty—this running up and down wasn't a hop, skip, and a jump thing. Plans had to be made weeks in advance, and much of the snow would be lost in transit. While this was the earliest form of long-haul transport, you can see the advantages of today's refrigerated trucking system.

Following in the tradition of Alexander the Great was Nero Claudius Caesar who reigned from A.D. 54 to 68. He too enjoyed ices, a Roman-style slush made from fresh snow and flavored with fruit, fruit and honey, or wines. While Nero fiddled around with his favorite recipes, slaves were again dashing up and down the Apennines mountains for snow. Nero, unfortunately, was considerably crankier than Alexander. If his slaves failed to come back with enough of the cold stuff, Nero would often get so peeved he had them beheaded. As one can surmise, turnover for ice slaves was brisk.

Once slave thought his number was up when he inadvertently spilled saltpeter on some of the snow, only to discover the juices and snow freezing quickly into a more solid slush. Alas, he received no credit for this (Blasius Villafranca did in the sixteenth century), and saltpeter has lost popularity for many sound health reasons. It is generally made from manure and its benefits remain questionable.

ICE CREAM MOMENT

Steve B., physicist, Akron, Ohio

During the Ohio winters of my youth, my mother made the most amazing concoction we used to call the Poor Kid's Ice Cream. My brothers and I would go outside as soon as it started snowing, bowl in hand, and "catch" snow falling from the sky. As soon as the bowl filled up we'd rush back inside, and Mom would weave her magic. Actually, it was pretty simple: she'd pour cold whole milk and at least a half-cup of sugar over the bowl of newly drifted snow, and the three of us would dive in with our spoons. It's hard to imagine how a cold, sweet dessert was so great during the winter, but it was. Maybe it was the half-cup of sugar.

THE ARAB INFLUENCE

The Arabs and Moors knew of the effect of salt on ice during their Spanish era (A.D. 711–1492).One of their written accounts of making ice is *Kitab Uyan al-Anba fi Tabaqat al-Atibba* (*Book Sources of Information on the Classes of Physicians*) in which the author, Ibn Abu Usaybi'a, described making artificial ice with cold water and saltpeter, a recipe he attributes to Ibn Bakhtawayhi. (An historian of medicine, Usaybi'a lived from A.D. 1230 to 1270.) No doubt this information about ice-making and perhaps a recipe or two for ices was passed along by Arabs to the many travelers to the Middle East during this time, including many explorers from Persia and India, plus the Polo triumvirate.

Many written recollections of those times have been preserved, some of which refer to the root of the sharbat bush, which was made into a cold drink. It is most likely that the Arabic word *sharbat* is the basis of the English word *sherbet*. The Arabs continue to create outstanding sherbets with exotic fruits that are both palate cleansing and utterly refreshing.

The most famous Persian ice cream is *sa'alub*, a very white dessert made from sa'alab, the ground-up root of an orchid flower. Its texture is rather elastic, and it is decidedly an acquired taste.

THE MEDICI STORY, BELIEVE IT OR NOT

So many myths abound about ice cream, but the stories are so interesting they're worth repeating with Ripley's caveat.

The use of artificial ice in the 1560s greatly helped the popularity of fruit ices and ice creams, but this advance came certainly *after* the time of Catherine de Medici, whose story still persists nonetheless.

The story, charming to be sure, alleges that Catherine de Medici introduced ice cream to the French court in 1533 when she married King Henry II. Catherine married

Henry when he was merely an up-and-coming royal (he was then only the Duke of Orleans), but she dutifully agreed to pack up, leave Italy, and move to Paris. She brought with her property, jewels, Italian style, and a complete staff including personal chefs.

The celebration of the royal wedding was so intense, the legend continues, that her Italian chefs created sumptuous meals every day for more than a month, each of which included a different flavor of "ice cream" made of "artificial ice" and fruit following the meal. Guests of the court were served this novel icy confection in a different way each evening for thirty-four days straight. And Baskin-Robbins thought it was clever with thirty-one . . .

ICE CREAM MOMENT

Robert Wemischner, author, *Vivid Flavors Cookbook*

When I think of ice cream, I think of Paris and 31, rue St. Louis en l'Ile. I first went to Paris in the 1970s, and the place for sorbet and ice cream was, and is, the fabled sorbetierre Berthilion. It was actually fun to wait in line, surrounded as we were by a mixture of the French *hoi polloi* and hippies from everywhere. Time seemed to fly as we waited for the opportunity to buy a single scoop of ice cream or sorbet for the then incredibly high price of $1 (U.S.). The reason? Exotic (to us) flavors like melon or cassis, café crunch or caramel, fraises des bois, noisette or praline, each with a touch of Paris in every bite. Summer or winter, hot or cold, the lines were always there. The salespeople and cashiers were equally crusty, but that never turned anyone away, because the raison d'être was fresh, beautiful, exquisite ice cream, made and sold within a few days, each with intense, intoxicating flavor and silky texture like nothing else.

THE FRENCH, WITH A LITTLE HELP FROM SPAIN . . .

French chefs, not to be outdone by their Italian counterparts, took function to a higher form, namely, molding the creams into *bombes glacés* made from concentric spheres that were pleated and molded into elaborate edible sculptures. (This was way before Jell-O molds.)

This frozen dessert was possible because of the Spaniard Blasius Villafranca, a physician who invented the first home ice cream freezer sometime during the 1560s. The "freezer" was a set of metal bowls with salted ice packed between them. (This technique is still serviceable, by the way.) As in Roman times, Villafranca sprinkled saltpeter on the cream prior to freezing. This is *not* suggested for modern usage.

Other European scientists were also exploring artificial ice and primitive forms of refrigeration. In his *Magnus Naturalis*, another Spaniard, Battista della Porta, noted in 1589 that various salts added to snow could produce very low temperatures. This quite remarkable observation would take many evolutions to become modern-day refrigeration, but it did a great deal even then to help preserve foods during a time when many people died from eating food that went bad. Pity the poor beefeater whose job it was to taste food for his king; if it was okay, the king dined, if not, the beefeater either got sick or died.

The French continued their passion for ice cream, which was celebrated by Louis XIV. His ardor was such that his renowned chef, Vatel, offered incredible ices following state meals. One guest wrote of an evening's splendor:

> Toward the end of the feast, his chef caused to be placed before each guest, in silver gilt cups, what was apparently a freshly laid egg, colored like those of Easter, but before the company had time to recover from their surprise at such a novelty at dessert, they discovered that the supposed eggs were delicious sweetmeats, cold and compact as marble.—Source unknown

The only emperor is the emperor of ice-cream.
—Wallace Stevens

BACK IN ENGLAND . . .

Richard the Lion-Hearted ate sherbet on the Holy Crusade in the East. Charles I of England wanted to keep ice cream a secret from his subjects, treating only his court to this dessert. He reportedly paid his chef five hundred pounds to keep his recipe a secret (or be beheaded) but, proving that what goes around comes around, Charles I himself was beheaded in 1649 instead of his chef, who was then able to share his deft abilities with ice cream and ices with anyone interested and willing to pay the price.

Although no records exist and no freezer pots remain in the memorabilia of King Charles I, we thought it was a clever way to tell you that even a story about ice cream can have a moral.

THE ETERNAL CAFÉ PROCOPE

What a pity this isn't a sin.
—Stendahl (1783–1842), upon his
first taste of ice cream

Ice cream was popular in Europe as early as the mid-1600s, as diarists and letter writers have attested, but it was in Paris that ices were being discovered as a premier dessert by the public fascinated with this novelty. No lust for only vanilla here, they wanted something different each visit.

Chefs obliged by expanding the repertoire of ices by adding fine French cream to make a dessert more similar to what we now call ice cream. The French, however, called this new variation milk ice or cream ice or butter ice, depending upon which of those ingredients was used.

By 1676, Paris was home to more than 250 shops selling ices and ice cream. The shops were so popular that France gave ice cream sellers official status as a trade guild, the true mark that a trade or skill was recognized by the French government.

When you visit Paris today, you can still enjoy sherbets and ice creams at Café Procope just as royalty and hoi polloi did in the seventeenth century. Located on the same site where it began in the late 1600s, Café Procope is on rue de l'Ancienne Comédie, across from the Comédie-Française. It was established not by a Frenchman, but a Sicilian, Procopio dei Coltelli, who offered fine coffees and chocolates and the Italian novelty then known simply as ices.

In 1768, *L'Art de Bien Faire des Glaces D'Office; ou Les Vrais Principes,* the first book devoted exclusively to ice cream recipes, was published, and ices and ice creams became available to the general public throughout France. No longer were these exquisite desserts accessible only to those who could afford Café Procope or to the aristocracy, who paid for the privilege of fine meals at the court by being witty and charming guests (sometimes a considerably higher price to pay).

L'Art is also evidence that the milk-based dessert, most likely was developed (if not originally conceived) by the French, who have a penchant for adding heavy cream to most everything. In the case of ice cream, this was a supremely wonderful idea.

A British cookbook that was published in 1718, *Mrs. Mary Eales Receipts,* included recipes for coarse ices, but it was not devoted exclusively to the confection as the French book was. Mrs. Eales often served Queen Anne, and her ices were well known at court receptions and lavish meals.

ITALIAN STYLE

Italy was also developing the ice cream dessert, most notably by a man named Tortoni, who in 1798 ran an ice cream shop at Number 10 Boulevard des Italiens. It was here that he devised his best known, and certainly most special of creations, Biscuit Tortoni, one of many molded desserts made with ice cream and ladyfinger-like biscuits and shaped into both ordinary and fanciful shapes.

THE NEW WORLD DISCOVERS ICE CREAM

During the 1700s, ice cream made its way across the Atlantic to the New World. While ice cream did not come over with the *Mayflower,* apparently a number of recipes did. In 1744, William Black, a guest of Governor Thomas Bladen of Maryland, wrote in his journal of a dinner he had at the Governor's mansion: ". . . after which came a Dessert no less Curious; Among the Rarities of which it was Compos'd, was some fine ice Cream which, with the Strawberries and Milk, eat most Deliciously." Governor Bladen, in fact, is often credited with the origin of the phrase "ice cream."

Following a trip to France in 1789, George Washington brought home two pewter pot freezers and later purchased a "Cream Machine for Making Ice" in Philadelphia, both used extensively at Mount Vernon for his favorite dessert. Bowls that were used for making ice cream are still in evidence at Mount Vernon. A tub or a pewter bowl was filled with ice and salt for freezing. A smaller bowl was used for the ingredients: milk, cream, eggs, sugar, and whatever flavorings were desired. One person, usually a slave, shook the small bowl, while another held the pot with the ice and salt. The resulting ice cream was a fairly heavy, textured product with no need for the gelatins, stabilizers, or other chemicals frequently found in commercial ice creams today.

It was an enormously popular dessert during the Revolutionary War, so much so that George Washington allegedly spent six shillings, and two pence—about two hundred dollars—on ice cream during one hot summer in 1790. That's Revolutionary War dollars—which were so solid they could sail across the Potomac River. Perhaps that overindulgent summer led poor George to his famous accessory: false teeth.

sabotiere

While President John Adams seemed to have skipped the passion for ices, President Thomas Jefferson loved the stuff and frequently served ice cream to his many guests. He was able to offer this treat because his magnificent home, Monticello, had an icehouse able to hold sixty-two wagon loads of ice harvested each year from the nearby Rivanna River during the winter. The icehouse kept everything from meat to butter well chilled.

His recipe is the first known American one for ice cream. The original, handwritten "receipt" for vanilla ice cream can be viewed in the Jefferson Papers Collection at the Library of Congress in Washington, D.C. Reprinted below, the recipe is still a viable way to make the confection, with or without Jefferson's version of a freezer, a *sabotiere*, which had no crank to turn it. A servant would grab the handle and turn the canister clockwise, then counterclockwise, for about ten minutes at a time.

THOMAS JEFFERSON'S VANILLA ICE CREAM

2 bottles of good cream $^{1}/_{2}$ lb. sugar
6 egg yolks   1 stick of vanilla

1. Mix yolks and sugar and put cream on a fire in a casserole, first putting in a stick of vanilla.
2. When near boiling, take it off the fire and pour gently into the mixture of eggs and sugar.
3. Stir it well.
4. Put it on the fire again, stirring it thoroughly with a spoon to prevent it from sticking to the casserole.
5. When near boiling, take it off and strain it through a towel.
6. Put it in an ice pail [*sabotiere*].
7. Then set it in ice for an hour before it is to be served. Put into the ice a handful of salt.
8. Put ice all around the ice pail, a layer of ice and a layer of salt for three layers.
9. Put salt on the cover of the ice pail and cover the whole pail with ice.
10. Leave it still for a quarter of an hour.
11. Then, turn the ice pail in the ice for ten minutes.
12. Open the ice pail to loosen the ice cream from the inside of the pail.
13. Close it and replace it in the ice. Open it from time to time to detach the ice from the sides.

14. When the ice cream is ready, stir it well with the spatula.
15. Put it into molds, justling it well down on the knee.
16. Put the molds back in ice until the moment of serving.
17. To serve, withdraw it and immerse the mold in warm water, turning it well till it comes out.
18. Serve it on a plate.

Or, get the premium French vanilla from the store, take it home, open up the box, and scoop it out for all; four steps, max.

First Lady Dolley served ice cream in the White House at President James Madison's second inaugural ball in 1812. Dolley added her magic touch by using strawberries from her own garden to make strawberry ice cream. This was not an entirely new recipe, as the Bladen party had also featured strawberry ice cream, sixty-eight years earlier, but it was rare enough to be considered novel by the inaugural ball guests several generations later.

It was another woman who helped bring ice cream to the masses, one Nancy Johnson of New Jersey, who invented the ice cream freezer with a revolving paddle inside a canister surrounded by space where one could place an ice-salt brine. Contrary to many accounts, she did indeed register her patent on September 9, 1843: U.S. Patent No. 3254. For two hundred dollars, she and her husband Walter assigned the rights to her invention to Williams and Company, which actively promoted her freezer.

> We dare not trust our wit for making our house pleasant
> to our friends so we buy ice cream.
> —Ralph Waldo Emerson, 1841

In 1848 two more ice cream–related patents were awarded, to businessman William H. Young and H.B. Masser, a newspaper editor.

Young's ice cream freezer, the second patented, had a moveable hand crank. It was made of a wooden pine pail with welded hoops and metal cylinders. By turning a handle, the operator churned the ice cream mix within a container that was submerged in a bucket of ice and salt.

Masser earned a patent for a freezer in which the ice was placed inside a narrow inner cylinder, allowing the ice cream mixture to be revolved around it in a larger cylinder. Although Masser's freezer wasn't really all that well designed, *Godey's Lady's Book* (a popular woman's magazine at the time), championed it, as did other publications. In fact, one issue of *Godey's* described hand-cranked freezer ice cream as "one of the necessities of life. A party without it would be like breakfast without bread or dinner without a roast."

The White Mountain Freezer Company, which is still in existence, was the first to market a freezer with two dashers with floats that turned in opposite directions when the cylinder was rotated. From 1843 until 1873 more than seventy designs for hand-cranked ice cream freezers were patented in the United States, and considerably more followed when electricity became available.

HARVESTING ICE

The study of ice played an important part in the popularity of ice cream and ices. Scientists throughout Europe were keenly interested in this, and in 1844, Thomas Masters

wrote *The Ice Book* in which he described in exhaustive detail the many different mixtures that could result from combining ice, acids, and salts.

Ice harvesting became a huge industry in the United States, and it was actually fairly simple to do. Ice harvesters depended upon strong workhorses to pull the heavy chunks of ice from ponds and strong men to carve out blocks of ice, scrape them clean, and plane them flat to standard sizes, usually a square block twenty-two inches thick although some slabs were up to thirty-six

Ice Breaker

inches thick. From 1806 through 1886, icehouses were everywhere, with some holding up to ninety thousand tons of ice.

It may be hard to imagine, but ice transport was a huge industry in the nineteenth century. Ice was shipped from the United States to the Caribbean, South America, and India, on both freighter and passenger ships, which used ice to keep food fresh and stored ice for future sale. Even when some of this precious cargo melted, there was still enough profit in delivering ice to make it very lucrative, thus creating a number of shipping magnates in the process.

With the invention of the icebox, the icehouse was no longer used at home, but some commercial ones remained even as late as the 1950s in some parts of the U.S.

The at-home icebox, usually no more than two feet square, provided consumers with a way to store this precious commodity and maintain the freshness of food for several days. No longer was it necessary to shop daily for perishables. This generated a new industry as hundreds of small entrepreneurs delivered ice to regular customers several times a week.

For a while, artificial ice took the place of true ice, but that too became a thing of the past as refrigeration became more efficient and more affordable.

The ice industry melted, and an entire new industry developed around the electric refrigerator. Although the industry continues to perfect the refrigerator unit, there is no question that today's refrigerators keep all foods fresher, longer. In addition, both stand-alone freezers and freezer units in refrigerators, have been improved to the point that they can automatically make ice, and keep foods frozen without freezer burn or unwanted melt-down. The frozen ice cream you buy today can be stored in the modern freezer unit for weeks and will be as delicious, and as solid, as the day you bought it.

JACOB FUSSELL, FATHER OF AMERICAN
ICE CREAM MANUFACTURERS

The continuing improvement of making ice no doubt helped boost the popularity of ices and ice creams in Europe. In America ice creams were still at-home recipes until the mid 1800s when necessity, that old mother of invention, led Baltimore entrepreneur Jacob Fussell into the ice cream business.

Looking for a way to sell surplus cream from his milk business, which began in 1851, Fussell started making some ice cream. It proved so popular, he decided to devote his entire dairy to ice cream production.

It always helps to have friends in high places, and one of Fussell's best friends, Abe Lincoln, awarded Fussell a contract to supply the Union troops with ice cream during the Civil War. Although he was an abolitionist and a Quaker, that did not stop Fussell from being a savvy businessman. (He tried to up the price to $1.25 a quart in Civil War dollars, but failed. Even given the enormous rates of inflation that marked the War Between the States, a buck and a quarter was very expensive.)

Shortly thereafter, in 1867, the centrifugal cream separator was invented, and Fussell's business really took off, providing him with the title the "father of the American ice cream industry."

AGNES MARSHALL OF LONDON

In England, Agnes B. Marshall, a professional cook who operated a kitchen equipment store and wrote extensively, published *The Book of Ices.* She catered, lectured, designed equipment (all with her name on it), and carried more than one thousand varieties and sizes of molds in conjunction with her books, *The Book of Ices* and *Fancy Ices.* (*The Book of Ices* was originally published in 1885 as *Ices, Plain and Fancy.*)

She patented an "ice cave," an ice cream freezer that was broad and shallow, unlike the style of the day, which was deep and narrow. She made only one trip to the United

Yours sincerely
Agnes B. Marshall

States, taking back with her some uniquely American recipes plus one novelty that stood her in good stead for her fancy ices: *sorbet à l'americaine.* She described it as . . .

> peculiarly interesting as it was first served in the cups or glasses formed of raw ice prepared in moulds in imitation of wine-glasses or cups. Its flavouring, when prepared in New York, is the sparkling California wine, Catawba, for which champagne is generally substituted in Europe. The moulds for making these ice cups or glasses consist of two parts, an inner and an outer cup, so that when fixed together they have the appearance of one cup; but between the two parts is a space which is filled with pure or coloured water. These are set in the ice-cave till the water is frozen; the ice-cups are then turned out of the moulds and used. The pretty effects which can be produced by real ice-glasses prepared in this way are so numerous that these moulds are now being used for sorbets of any kind.

(The Catawba wine was actually from the Ohio River Valley. The ice cups were a sound ecological invention; they disappeared along with the sorbet, eliminating the cost and effort of cleanup.)

Marshall, the most renowned cookery entrepreneur of London, died at the age of fifty in 1905, but her school survived her until the early 1950s. Her many hundreds of ice cream molds have become collectible by ice cream memorabilia enthusiasts.

BAKED ALASKA MAKES ITS DEBUT

Back in the United States, ices and sherbets were considered exceptional desserts, and in New York both Delmonico's and Sherry's restaurants made a specialty of these unique items. Charles Ranhofer, Delmonico's chef from 1862 to 1894, was well known for his ice cream desserts and is credited with inventing Baked Alaska.

His recipe called for a tall cone, half of banana ice cream and half of vanilla ice cream, set into a round cake, slightly hollowed out, and lined with apricot marmalade. The dessert was kept frozen until the last minute, then covered with meringue, browned quickly under the broiler, and served immediately.

Allegedly this dessert was created to commemorate the purchase of Alaska from Russia in 1867 by William Henry Seward, but it was often called a Baked Florida (to add an aura of confusion to an otherwise popular dessert).

No one, however, can deny that Ranhofer was a stellar chef. He did veer off to the occasional oddity, like asparagus ice cream and truffle (mushroom not chocolate). Each to his own taste, perhaps, although it must be mentioned that a Victorian meal often ended with vegetables, sometimes savory and sometimes, as Agnes Marshall and Ranhofer were known to do, made like desserts. Tomato or cucumber ices were very popular, and quite refreshing.

SUNDAES AND SODAS

Michigan State University students in 1982 constructed the world's largest sundae, containing 15,000 pounds of Friendly Ice Cream Corporation ice cream, 120 pounds of chocolate syrup, 25 pounds of Reese's Pieces, and 50 pounds of whipped topping.

How many people it took to devour it is not recorded.

Two special ice cream desserts were developed in the late 1800s: the sundae and the soda. The ice cream soda is sometimes attributed to Fred Sanders of Detroit. Sanders sold a beverage of sweet cream, carbonated water, and fruit juice, but in the hot summer of 1879, his cream turned sour and was unusable. What to do? Fred reached for some ice cream, and history was made.

Another legend, and the one most ice cream historians agree to, attributes the invention of the ice cream soda to soda water concessionaire Robert M. Green. Green, who worked in Philadelphia, sold a mixture of carbonated water, cream, and syrup. One day, like Sanders, he ran out of cream and substituted ice cream, hoping customers wouldn't notice. They did, and to his surprise, Green's sales went from six dollars to six hundred dollars per day.

Despite their refreshing taste, ice cream sodas were considered by some to be too pleasurable for the Christian Sabbath, and the local blue laws of the Midwest outlawed serving sodas on Sunday. Evanston, Illinois, previously known as Heavenstown, a fitting name for so heavenly a drink, can lay claim for legislating against the "Sunday Soda Menace" in the 1890s.

Customer George Hallauer of Two Rivers, Wisconsin, asked the soda jerk at Ed Berner's soda fountain for a little chocolate syrup on his ice cream, thus creating an all-new dish soon called a Sunday. Ice cream parlor owner George Giffy of Manitowoc, Wisconsin, decided to change the spelling to "sundae" after recognizing the growing popularity of putting chocolate syrup on ice cream. He advertised his renamed concoction heavily and soon "sundae" replaced "Sunday" and Giffy scooped up a winner.

> *Cones are composed of many a vitamin.*
> *My lap is not the place to bitamin.*
> —"Family Reunion," by Ogden Nash,
> in *Verses From 1929 On*

ICE CREAM MOMENT

G. Simpson, teacher, Raleigh, North Carolina

Different people have different styles for eating an ice cream cone. Some make it a science, others an art; some just plunge right in without any sense of direction. For example, I like to lick the ice cream scoop from left to right and suck in the melting top. My sister always licked from bottom to top, rotating the cone counterclockwise. Some people actually bite into ice cream and chew it.

Cone choices are important, too. Some people like wafer cones, others like molasses or dark cones, and still others like cones dipped in chocolate.

Of course, people who like ice cream in a cup are generally viewed by cone people as sorta picky. Maybe even fastidious. But I maintain that what is less messy is less fun.

I've always wondered whatever happened to my grade school girlfriend Sylvia. No matter how often she had an ice cream cone, no matter where she ate it, she always made the same mistake over and over again. She'd start at the *tip* of the cone and eventually, the scoop of ice cream would topple and she'd have to catch it with her hand and plop it back on, or the scoop would fall completely off, leaving her with just a smidge of ice cream on the cone and a mound of green mint ice cream lying split-splat on the sidewalk. This bull-headedness of her, to not want to try to eat the cone from top to bottom instead of the other way around, just could not sink into her head. I've wondered for years whether she was that way her whole life or just with ice cream cones. She's probably a rocket scientist now.

Experts Waffle on the Cone Inventor

The ice cream cone is the only ecologically sound package known.
It is the perfect package.
  —"60 Minutes," quoting of U.S. Health, Education
  and Welfare official in 1969.

Who invented the ice cream cone is a story still being contested. It is a fact that in the late 1800s, paper cones and metal containers were popular in France and edible cornets were used in England. Edible waffle cones were used in Germany by 1900.

Charles Ranhofer, who created the Baked Alaska, lists a recipe in his cookbook *The Epicurean* (1894) for rolled waffle cornets filled with whipped cream, most likely based on an English recipe for brandy snaps. This appears to be the earliest recipe for a cone-like confection. This brings up a point cone connoisseurs like to mention: Cones came in two distinct shapes, a rolled wafflelike confection and a molded cone that looks like a cup.

Italo Marchiony, like a lot of Italians in New York, peddled ice cream via pushcart. In the late 1890s he sold his ices and ice creams with European paper cones, but they were messy. Next, he tried glass containers, but they required constant cleanup. He knew the key to better sales was an edible cone. His answer was to develop a mold for a container, and in 1903 he applied for a patent for his design, which was for a small cup with very small handles, not a waffle cone.

A year later, a version of the waffle ice cream cone was introduced during the 1904 World Exposition in St. Louis. What is not clear is who introduced it.

Ice cream was an enormous hit at the fair, which had more than fifty booths selling ice cream either exclusively or along with other food products. Together they sold more than five thousand gallons per day throughout the event. This was fortunate for fairgoers, who came in record numbers despite the unusually hot temperatures of the summer of 1904. Everyone was looking for something cool to eat, and there were many ice cream vendors there to sell this still-novel dessert.

While Marchiony was in New York, Charles Menches was selling a variety of foods, including ice cream served on plates, at his large booth in St. Louis. Soon the demand for dishes outstripped his staff's ability to clean them. Allegedly, a woman employee of his reached for a waffle cookie at the booth next to them and rolled it around the ice cream, not realizing at first that it would drip through.

Another legend is that Ernest A. Hamwi, who sold those waffle cookies, Persian *zalabias*, created a functional cone by folding the cookie into a conical shape and pinching the bottom into a point. He called it "The World's Fair Cornucopia." Still another legend says that it was not Hamwi, but his employee, Nick Kabbaz who came up with the idea and that Hamwi simply took the concept for his own.

Ultimately St. Louis went on to become the cone capital of America, and at the industry's height in 1924, more than 245 million cones were made that year.

So who invented the ice cream cone? Was it the English, French, or German chefs and inventors who created various forms of cones years before the World's Fair? Was it Marchiony, the Italian immigrant to the United States who died with his patent mired in legal technicalities and still pending? Or was it Nick Kabbaz, a Syrian immigrant whose original idea may have been taken by his boss but who, undaunted, went on to head a successful cone-making firm?

Was it the boss, Hamwi, whose engineering skills built cone-making machinery that enabled his company to outlast bankruptcy and legal maneuvering to be a legacy for his family? Or was it an unnamed woman working at the World's Fair booth of Charles Menches?

Want to make the question more complicated? Other claimants to the creation have surfaced: Turkish immigrant David Avayou and Lebanese immigrant Abe Doumar each claimed to have created the original recipe for the waffle ice cream cone. (Doumar's sons continued his tradition with an ice cream stand known as *Doumar's*, which stood for many years in Norfolk, Virginia.)

The jury is still out, but cones are still an important player in the $10-billion ice cream industry. Innovations have created sugar, wafer, and waffle styles. For those who can't leave a good thing alone, one can dip the cone into a vat of chocolate and garnish it with candy sprinkles or chopped nuts.

Vendors love cones, too. A paper bowl and plastic spoon can cost more than five cents, require disposal, and raise recycling concerns; a cone costs less than two cents, and even if it breaks, it's still edible. If you don't want to eat the crunchy, harder bottom, it is genuinely biodegradable; onto the compost pile it goes.

AMERICAN INGENUITY AND COMPETITION SPUR GROWTH OF ICE CREAM

The twenties brought many ice cream innovations. Commercially, the most important development was the air-inject freezer, which added as much as 60 percent air into the ice cream mix.

When ice cream is whipped by hand, air does seep into the mixture, making the ice cream about 10 to 15 percent air. The air-inject freezer took this natural step a considerable distance. Consequently, commercial ice creams owe their light texture to being nearly two-thirds air.

Clarence Vogt of Kentucky invented the first successful continuous freezer in 1926, enabling ice cream makers to mass produce their product. In Vogt's machine, one poured the ingredients in at one end of the machine and ice cream came out the other end. This led to true mass marketing, including the social "pub" of the 1920s through the 1950s—the ice cream parlor.

The twenties brought new taste sensations for commercially produced ice creams, including the Eskimo Pie, created by Christian Nelson in Iowa in 1921, and the Good Humor sucker, patented by Harry Burt, Sr., of Ohio in 1923. While the Eskimo Pie has no patent and many imitators, the Good Humor bar continues, under the parentage of Breyer's Ice Cream.

That same year, H. P. Hood of Boston made a tub-shaped paper cup that he introduced at the National Ice Cream Convention in Cleveland. Although you can understand why he wanted to retain the original name, the Hoodsie, it was subsequently renamed the Dixie Cup in 1924 and has been called that ever since. The same cup, lightly waxed and usually white, is still used along with a little wooden spoon with pointed scoops at either end, to serve ice cream at snack shops everywhere. The Dixie cups, which often included inserts decorated with celebrities, have become sought-after collectibles.

In 1923, a form of sherbet on a stick, known as the Popsicle, was developed by Frank Epperson of California. Epperson originally called his confection an Epsicle, and for a little while he and Harry Burt, Sr., battled in their efforts for market share. They eventually compromised, giving Epperson the sherbet market with Popsicle and Burt the ice cream market with the Good Humor Bar, complete with a flotilla of vans clinking up and down the streets of America well into the 1950s. Both desserts are still popular and sold everywhere frozen desserts can be found. Breyer's now owns Burt's bar, and Nestlé owns Epperson's; yet, fortunately, barely an ingredient has changed since the two men created their frozen confections more than seventy years ago.

"I Scream, You Scream, We All Scream for Ice Cream"
—popular song in 1927 written by
Billy Moll and Howard E. Johnson

Tin Pan Alley responded to the popularity of ice cream with songs like this and the immortal "I Scream, You Scream, We All Scream for Ice Cream." (*Eskimo Pie Corp.*)

An example of manipulating the standard ice cream recipe was the invention of a machine that created "soft ice cream." Tom Carvel invented and patented an electric freezer in 1939 that froze the ice cream at a slightly higher temperature, added more air into the mixture, and created a sweeter, softer ice cream that spawned a whole industry of stand-alone counters, making Carvel and others millionaires.

Another pioneer in the soft-serve industry was F. J. "Grandpa" McCullough and his son H. A. (Alex), proprietors of the Homemade Ice Cream Company, which they opened in 1927 in their hometown of Davenport, Iowa. Deciding that the suburbs were the future, they moved during the early 1930s to a building they had purchased in Green River, Illinois, that had been a cheese factory.

Their first ice cream recipe included 10 percent butterfat, milk solids, sweetener, and stabilizer, which they combined and processed into a batch freezer holding about forty quarts. When the ice cream reached 23° F, a worker opened a spigot in the freezer and the soft product spilled out into three-gallon tubs which were covered and placed in a deep freezer at −10° F and later delivered to retail customers.

When the ice cream shop operator was ready to serve the rock-hard ice cream, he placed it in a dipping cabinet and warmed it to 5° F. Therefore, ice cream was frozen solid for the convenience of the ice cream maker and seller, not the customer. The McCulloughs began to think that their ice cream really tasted best at that original 23° F temperature. As a result, they started to experiment with mix formulas. The mechanically-minded Alex began to tinker with freezer parts to change the way ice cream was made, but although the idea was great, there was a real problem in finding a freezer to make mass produced soft-serve ice cream a practical reality.

Meanwhile, the McCulloughs wanted to test-market the softer confection and asked Sherb Noble, who owned several ice cream stores, to stage a campaign, "All You Can Eat for 10 Cents" to introduce his new concept. On August 4, 1938, Noble did just that at his Kankakee, Illinois, store, Sherb's Ice Cream Shop. This campaign brought an explosion of enthusiasm: one thousand six hundred servings during the two-hour promotion.

Sherb Noble was rewarded for his enthusiasm with the first official Dairy Queen store, which opened on June 22, 1940, in Joliet, Illinois. Noble grew along with the company as a store owner for more than fifty-two years; even in semi-retirement, he owned seven stores.

The success of Dairy Queen's version of soft-serve was due to a new type of freezer developed and patented by Harry M. Oltz, who was the "Hamburger King" of Hammond, Illinois, where he owned a burger restaurant and custard stand. He sold the McCulloughs the rights to the machine for areas of the country west of the Mississippi River and for Illinois and Wisconsin. Oltz then developed AR-TIK Systems, Inc., for similar soft-cone operations in the southern and southeastern states. His estate's interests were acquired during the 1960s by International Dairy Queen, thus bringing the company back full circle.

Today, the Cone with the Curl on Top is available at more than 5,200 Diary Queen stores throughout the United States and Canada and in 175 stores in twelve other countries, even Japan and China, where milk desserts are still novel.

Dairy Queen is one of several all-American companies owned by International Dairy Queen, Inc. (IDQ) including Orange Julius, Golden Skillet, and Karmelkorn Shoppes, Inc. The IDQ was purchased in 1997 by one of Warren Buffet's companies, Berkshire-Hathaway, Inc., which plans to keep all the soft-serve ice cream favorites just the way they've been since 1940.

HOWARD JOHNSON AND THE FIRST "28 FLAVORS"

Born in Boston in 1896, and relatively uneducated (he never even reached high school), Howard Johnson first began his entrepreneurial climb in 1925 at a Wollaston, Massachusetts, drugstore soda fountain. Looking for a way to make the soda fountain different and attract more customers, he developed the then novel concept of multiple flavors—twenty-eight of them.

He took his concept further than the single soda fountain and began operating ice cream stands throughout the greater Boston area, with each of these featuring the highly unusual, but definitely eye-catching, color orange. He sold a phenomenal fourteen thousand cones during one hot summer day at his stand on Wollaston Beach, just a glimpse of the success he was soon to have nationwide.

Johnson opened his first restaurant in a new bank building in nearby Quincy in 1929 and began to franchise his name in 1935 when he convinced Reginald Sprague to open an ice cream stand and restaurant in Orleans on Cape Cod. Although owned by Sprague, the restaurant featured both Johnson's name and his products, and was so popular it led to an explosion of franchisees—130 restaurants by 1940.

The Pennsylvania Turnpike helped make Howard Johnson rich. He understood the coming power of the highway system and won exclusive catering rights on thousands of miles of highways in the eastern United States. He built many of his famous orange motels kitty-corner to each other on the same highway, to attract customers driving in either direction, making it very easy for them to stop off for his famous ice cream, or stay overnight.

By the 1970s, there were more than one thousand Howard Johnson restaurants and five hundred motels. Johnson died in 1972, prior to the company being sold several times. Although Howard Johnson hotels and motels still abound, most of their restaurants have eliminated the menu of ice creams, a decided loss to those who remember the fun of having such dramatic choices to make. But, as is always the case in American business, there is always someone in the background ready to cash in on an original idea.

MR. BASKIN, MEET MR. ROBBINS

If you can't lick 'em, join 'em, might have been the motto of Irv Robbins and Burt Baskin, brothers-in-law who originally operated competing ice cream stores in Glendale, California, during the forties.

Baskin, no newcomer to exotic ice creams, had been creating ice cream flavors since his navy days in the New Hebrides when he used local fruits to make ice creams for his fellow sailors. A PX operator, he managed to obtain an ice cream freezer from a very cooperative supply officer.

In 1945, Robbins opened the Snowbird, with twenty-one exotic flavors. and was soon urged to join competitor Burt Baskin to form Baskin-Robbins. He did so in 1946, and the team quickly opened six successful stores in three years.

Their concept of "31 flavors" was born during 1953, based on the idea of offering a different flavor for each day of the month. The variety and choice was innovative and exciting and quickly caught the attention of the public, who made the new ice cream store the "in spot," knowing that they could always get strawberry, vanilla, or chocolate.

Among the "firsts" the firm introduced was a light, 93 percent fat-free ice cream in 1990. In 1991, it was the first retail ice cream group to introduce fat-free frozen dairy desserts, and a nonfat soft-serve ice cream debuted in 1995. Its all-natural low-fat and nonfat frozen yogurts have been store fixtures since 1987.

The firm, now a wholly owned subsidiary of Allied-Domecq, has more than 3,500 retail stores that each rotate more than one hundred flavors a year, always maintaining the world-renowned minimum of "31 flavors."

Baskin died in 1967 at age fifty-four, and Robbins retired as chairman in 1978.

AMERICAN ICE CREAM AFTER THE WAR

Throughout World War II, GI's were given tons (literally) of ice cream by an increasingly powerful dairy industry. In fact, during 1943, the U.S. Air Force was the single largest producer of ice cream in the world, producing and distributing ice cream in quantities greater than any other commercial manufacturer up to that time.

Following the development of increasingly sophisticated and efficient electric refrigerators with the then-unique built-in freezer, take-home ice cream soared in sales because consumers finally had a reliable way to preserve "store bought" ice cream.

Along with all-electric homes and a slew of new gadgets, the 1950s saw a culinary revolution as food manufacturers sought to increase the shelf life of their products with additives, preservatives, and other "ives." Ice cream changed from a fresh fruit-flavored frozen milk product to an airy dessert known more for its cool smoothness than its delectable taste. Some of the additives used, like gelatin added to sherbet or flour and whole eggs added to ice cream, were fairly harmless. Other then little-understood chemicals, however, did much to enhance shelf life, but we are only now discovering what they're doing to our personal "shelf life."

Fortunately, technology has a plus side, and by the 1960s, new at-home ice cream machines, both hand-cranked and electric versions, were available everywhere and reasonably priced. Now anyone could easily make ice cream and sherbet at home. The real bonus of these machines is that they make desserts that are genuinely delicious because consumers use fresh ingredients and eat the result immediately.

That is not to say that some traditional ice cream vendors do not exist. Italian gelati stores are commonplace; commercial fruit and cream or fruit ices are everywhere; and many ice cream makers, both regional and national, have stuck to the age-old formula of milk, cream, sugar, fresh flavorings, eggs, and a dash of salt. To these stalwart saviors, we shout, "Hallelujah and pass the Cherry Garcia, please."

Collecting Ice Cream Memorabilia
● ● ● ● ● ● ● ● ● ● ● ● ● ● ● ● ● ● ●

One of my personal theories about "stuff" is that one is an item, two is a set, and three is a collection, and usually requires dusting. That theory is completely ignored by members of The Ice Screamers, for whom collecting memorabilia related to America's favorite dessert is just plain fun.

The Ice Screamers meet in Lancaster, the heart of Pennsylvania dairy country, every June for their annual convention, an event that gives members a chance to display an incredible assortment of ice cream-themed items. Among the more popular collectibles are hand-cranked freezers, hundreds of styles of pewter ice cream molds, and ice cream scoops which are the number one collectible among The Ice Screamers. (Some scoops date to the late 1800s and early 1900s.)

Paper ephemera, which is easy to collect and to store, has many fans, especially those unable to display one hundred crank freezers at home. Paper ephemera includes such products as posters, greeting cards, postcards, Valentine's Day cards, magazine covers featuring ice cream-related items, and sheet music of the more than one thousand ice cream songs that have been written, if not recorded, about our favorite dessert.

Who could pass up collecting sheet music of titles like "Ice Cream Alley Blues" by William Alexander Couser, "Ice Cream and Lies" by Bonnet, Jones, Libersher, Forden, and Rutledge, or my personal favorite, "Ice Cream All Over His Moustache," by Colin Peter Palmer. While only a few top people have written about ice cream, notably Jerry Bock and Sheldon M. Harnick for their Broadway show *She Loves Me*, both the American Society of Composers, Authors, and Publishers and Broadcast Music, Inc. list several hundred odes to America's favorite dessert that have actually been recorded.

The soda fountain has generated many collections (some of the fountain bar itself), advertising art, straws from famous soda fountains and straw holders, and ice cream trays which were used to serve treats from the fountain.

Everything about soda fountains is collected from signs for products to shop signs; the glass or metal serving glasses and dishes for sundaes, milk shakes and banana splits, to costumes of soda jerks, to the machinery to make it all happen: milk shake machines, soda dispensers, and syrup jars.

One collector has more than four hundred ice cream cartons from various companies, including items from 130 foreign countries. Dixie lids are also a hot find. From 1928 until the 1950s, the Dixie Cup division of the American Can Company released several series of pictures that were placed under a thin piece of waxed paper under the lid for all the ice cream cups it sold. The series included circus animals, movie stars, cowboy heroes, baseball players, World War II figures, and United States Presidents.

Another collector has amassed more than one thousand ice cream poems and is planning an anthology. Still another collects wind-up toy ice cream trucks, so popular in the 1930s.

The Ice Screamers began with a meeting of ice cream collectors in Chicago in 1982, including fifty-five-year-veteran of the ice cream industry and group founder-president Ed Marks. The organization's goal is "recapturing the fun and magic of those old ice cream parlor–soda fountain days" and adding this vibrant part of history to the cultural lexicon. It has grown from a small group to include more than seven hundred members, who produce a quarterly newsletter, "The Ice Screamer," which prints information on collectibles, memorabilia, ads, and news and reviews of items of interest to these inveterate collectors. The Ice Screamers officers organize the annual convention, answer questions about the art and science of ice cream and its many collectibles, and plan and coordinate related events for the membership.

The Ice Screamers is more than just a group of collectors, for many of its members are serious historians who study the ice cream industry from its early beginnings to the present day and who are staunch preservationists of what they view as a true slice of Americana.

If you'd like to join the fun, or learn more about collecting ice cream memorabilia, write to The Ice Screamers, P.O. Box 465, Warrington, PA 18976. Dues are $15 per year.

THE QUEEN OF SODA FOUNTAINS

Speaking of ice cream memorabilia mania, here's an amusing anecdote from William J. Birnes of Los Angeles, California:

It's hard not to appreciate the functional beauty of well-designed soda fountains that became the social centers of American small towns and villages around the turn of the century. These ornate dispensers of ice cream desserts—each sundae or shake made just slightly different because they were *hand-made*—became altars to a way of life gradually displaced when life speeded up too fast for the slow pure pleasure of a sundae on a Saturday afternoon.

I've always wanted one, so when I read about a little village near Philadelphia where a century–old pharmacy and ice cream parlor was holding an estate auction of its original fixtures, I dropped everything and made the three hour drive from my home in New Nesanic Station, New Jersey.

By the time my wife and I arrived, the place was crawling with antique dealers who presumed the pickings were going to be easy and had probably already presold much of what they were going to buy. The inventory was glorious: a 1940s Wurlitzer jukebox, a set of caned bentwood ice cream parlor chairs, an original frog mannequin for frog-in-the-throat drops, and my heart's desire, a 1903 Hires Root Beer soda fountain. *Magnificent!*

The Wurlitzer was the first big piece to go in a bidding frenzy with so many paddles in the air at the same time the place looked like a national political party convention. The frog mannequin almost started a war among the bidders. Other pieces came and went at prices way beyond any Keynesian logic.

But, where was the soda fountain? Why was the auctioneer waiting?

By the time the lengthening shadows had crept across the back lawn and the auctioneer switched to portable lights, the summer heat had exacted its toll. Crisply starched shirts were now wilted, stained with perspiration; wet towels were hung around necks like white scarves around toffs at a formal event; and heads nodded listlessly.

Driven by hunger and thirst, the group had succumbed to the temptation of ice cold Cokes and steaming hot dogs out of the cart which perfumed the air. Paddles became swatters as the mosquitoes attacked. The auctioneer seemed to be looking for something, someone. The auction was breaking up. Had this all been a cruel hoax? Had I been lured to this spot as food for mosquitoes and nothing else?

"Well, we can't wait any longer," the auctioneer finally said, directing the loblolly boys to wrest my coveted soda fountain from its corner to the auction stage and plug the ancient cloth wire into an electric socket.

Like fireworks on the Fourth of July, the huge Hires ball came aglow, and suddenly, magically, it was as if I slipped through a seam in time and was at the St. Louis World's Fair in 1904 when, the auctioneer assured us, this Hires Root Beer fountain had first appeared. There were muted oohs and ahs.

"Anybody got a thousand for this rose marble original Hires Root Beer Fountain from the St. Louis World's Fair?"

Silence.

"Let's start at seven-fifty," the auctioneer said, his voice still full of confidence belying the lateness of the hour.

Silence.

"Six? Six will get us going. Do I hear six hundred?"

"I'll go no lower than five, five hundred. Five hundred for a piece of American history. Five hundred for the very soda fountain where your grandparents sat at the Saint LOU-IEEEE World's Fair."

I could not raise my hand.

"I'm not going to let this beauty go. Boys, pack it up," he said.

"Two-fifty," a familiar voice called out. Who said that? The voice was indeed mine.

"Two fifty?" the auctioneer said with a sneer. "Two hundred and fifty dollars for the very soda fountain your grandparents went courting at in St. Louis? OK, two fifty, I'm all for charity," he announced. "Who's in at two seventy-five?"

Nobody. Silence.

"You're going to let this go on one bid for two hundred and fifty?" he asked the crowd. Silence. "Going once," he rapped his gavel.

"Two seventy-five," a voice called out of the darkness.

"Do I hear three?" The auctioneer asked.

"Three," someone else called out.

"How about three fifty?"

"Going once at three."

"Three twenty-five," I called out.

"Three fifty again? Do I hear three fifty?"

"Three fifty," a bidder out of the darkness shouted.

The chase was up.

"Four. Someone give me four hundred," the auctioneer cried, his spirit restored by the contest.

"Three seventy-five," I called out.

"I want four," he said, but there was only silence.

"Three eighty," my unseen adversary called out.

"Three eighty-five," I answered. And on and on we went, escalating by pathetic five-dollar increments until the bidding finally broke through the fours.

"Four fifty," I called out. Nothing would keep me from this soda fountain and that incredibly magnificent glowing translucent ball perched atop like a monument to a life once enjoyed but now gone forever.

"Four fifty once," the auctioneer cried. He was as anxious as all of us to get this over with.

"Four fifty twice."

SLAM went the gavel. "You-uuuuuu bought it!" he sung triumphantly like a cry of victory. "Sold at four hundred and fifty dollars."

Like a driver in a Monte Carlo start, I was at my Land Cruiser turning over the engine as the gavel went down. I rolled back the canvas tarp, backed it over the soft lawn to the table, and lowered the transom. This was my moment. Then, while the line of winners queued up at the cashier's table, my wife and I unplugged the frayed cloth wire and stared in disbelief at all the different parts of this fountain. No big deal, just take out a few screws, wrap the pieces in the moving canvas we brought, load her up, and drive her home.

No big deal at all . . . until we tried lifting the first piece: pure rose marble quarried from the hills just north of Rome. It just wouldn't budge. I looked around in desperation for the loblolly boys, but they had disappeared. My wife and I strained again and again, but nothing budged. My wife had tears in her eyes; not even her renowned furniture moving skills would suffice.

We sat there on the grass staring at the trophy we had bought, but could not move. The huge chunks of marble looked like the stones of the pyramids and seemed just as heavy.

My Hires Root Beer soda fountain, *my* soda fountain, lay in structural disassembly on the wet grass of a summer night far from home. I had bought it, I had touched it, but could not lift it. My dreams of a soda fountain were not only not to be, but I was still out the money.

"You folks like that?" a very deep voice from a very wide, no-necked individual said standing over us.

"Yeah, I came all the way from New Jersey to bid for it," I said.

"So did I," he said. "But got here late."

"Say," I began. "Maybe you could give us a hand here. You know, maybe lift this thing up together."

"Got a better idea," he said. "I'm a beer distributor in Trenton. Had a hankering for something like this ever since my grandparents showed me a picture of it in the drug store they owned. So I won't help you lift it. But I'll give you more than double what you paid." He took a roll of bills out of his deep overalls pocket. "Spoke to the cashier. She said you paid four hundred and fifty. Here's," and he began to peel off fifties and then hundreds. "Here's one thousand. Take it or leave it." And he looked down at the huge rose marble slabs that were the sides of the soda fountain. "And I mean leave it."

I ran my hands over the Hires ball. Ran my hands over it again and again.

"Take it," my wife said, and the beer distributor handed over hundreds and fifties.

I visited the soda fountain once or twice at its new home in downtown Trenton. I sat at the counter, had a real root beer, and looked lovingly at what I once owned for about fifteen minutes.

It was his trophy now, this explosion of crystal and marble topped by the crown of a Hires globe. And it worked. I had just about the best root beer you ever tasted. He floated a scoop of homemade vanilla ice cream—yes, he made his own ice cream—on top of it and I had my favorite black cow.

Was the longing for this queen of soda fountains greater than the delight of a soda I could enjoy any time I wished? Maybe after all it was the black cow that was what I wanted. I sure enjoyed it, and best of all, I got it for free. Later on, my wife revealed that we didn't even have enough in the bank to cover the original bid of $450. The beer distributor from Trenton not only saved us a bundle in late charges, he put us in the black. Thanks, guy.

© 1986 KFS Inc./Fleischer Studios Inc.

Ice Cream Facts and Trivia to Fascinate Your Friends

Who Eats What

1. The average number of licks it takes to eat a single-scoop ice cream cone is about fifty.
2. Ice cream is a $10.7-billion industry.
3. The north central states have the highest per capita consumption of ice cream (46.8 quarts).
4. More ice cream is sold on Sundays than on any other day of the week.
5. The most popular ice cream topping is still chocolate.
6. One cup of hard ice cream contains 270 calories, 5 grams of protein, 14 grams of fat, 8.9 grams of saturated fat, 32 grams of carbohydrates, and 176 milligrams of calcium.

Data for "Ice Cream Facts and Trivia" are provided by the International Ice Cream Association and the International Dairy Foods Association, Washington, D.C., from statistics provided by the U.S. Department of Agriculture. Nutritive values from the Home and Garden Bulletin #72 from the Superintendent of Documents, U.S. Government Printing Office.

7. Nearly one-third of American households consume at least one gallon of ice cream and related frozen desserts every two weeks.

8. A 10-ounce chocolate milkshake contains 355 calories, 9 grams of protein, 8 grams of fat, 4.8 grams of saturated fat, 60 grams of carbohydrates, and 374 milligrams of calcium.

9. July is National Ice Cream Month. The third Sunday of July is officially National Ice Cream Day.

10. A cup of sherbet has 270 calories, 2 grams of protein, 4 grams of fat, 2.4 grams of saturated fat, 59 grams of carbohydrates, and 103 milligrams of calcium.

11. What sells the most? Regular ice cream accounts for 56 percent of the market, the largest share of frozen dessert sales.

12. Reduced-fat, low-fat, and nonfat ice cream accounts for 25 percent of the market.

13. Frozen yogurt accounts for only 10 percent of the frozen dessert market, followed by water ices (aka sorbets) at 4 percent, and sherbet at 3 percent; the remaining 2 percent include rice, soy, and tofu-based frozen desserts.

14. The top three flavors sold in United States supermarkets are vanilla, chocolate, and Neapolitan.

15. The top three frozen yogurt flavors are vanilla, fruit (except strawberry), and chocolate. Strawberry is a flavor unto itself and number five.

16. The top three flavors of syrup toppings are hot fudge, chocolate fudge, and caramel.

17. The total production in the United States for all frozen desserts was 1.5 billion gallons in 1996. That's 23.4 quarts per person for a total retail value of nearly $11 billion.

18. Finland ranks second to the United States in per capita production of ice cream and frozen desserts, with 38.13 pints per person; Denmark is third, with 34.76 pints per person.

19. California produces the largest volume of ice cream and related frozen desserts in the United States; Pennsylvania, Indiana, Texas, Ohio, and Illinois are next.

20. The average shelf price per gallon of ice cream in 1996 was $5.84.

21. Portland, Oregon, ranks first in supermarket sales of ice cream with 2.87 gallons per capita, followed by St. Louis (2.65 gallons) and Seattle (2.64 gallons).

22. In 1996, 442 packaged ice cream and related products and 142 frozen novelty products were introduced to the market.

23. Over 98 percent of all packaged super premium ice cream is sold in pint-sized containers and more than 90 percent of all packaged premium ice cream and frozen yogurt comes in half-gallon containers.
24. Super premium ice cream is most commonly found in homes where there are no children.
25. More quarts of ice cream are sold in medium-size cities and more pints are sold in very large cities.
26. Children ages two to seventeen and adults forty-five and over eat the most ice cream per person.
27. Japan imports 30 percent of all U.S. ice cream shipments abroad for a total of $34.9 million, making it the single largest market for U.S. frozen dessert exports during the last three years.

ICE CREAM CONCERTO

Mexican musician Roberto Limon, interested in performing music that was "purely American," got a real taste of the United States when Meyer Kupferman* presented him with "Ice Cream Concerto" in 1992.

Limon and his Atril Cinco Ensemble Mexicano Contemporaneo premiered the concerto in 1992 in Mexico City as part of Mexico's Fifteenth International Festival of New Music.

The work is designed in two large movements and is intended for performance as a chamber work without a conductor. It is an ice cream game of eleven whistles and a quica drum, bringing the concerto to an arresting close.

The poetic and philosophical undertones, Kupferman said, are drawn from Wallace Stevens' poem, "The Emperor of Ice Cream" "touching on those complex rituals of humor, games and love . . . the true reality of the artist."

*Kupferman is professor emeritus of the music school of Sarah Lawrence College where he taught for more than forty-three years, and has written several symphonies, concertos for violin, cello, and clarinet, film scores, and ballet scores for José Limon and Martha Graham. He currently writes music full time.

The premiere performance in Mexico was enthusiastically received and not without charm. Near the very end of the performance, a local ice cream vendor, in full regalia, came onstage ringing his bells against the music of the concerto. He then began to offer composer Kupferman, the members of the orchestra, and then the audience ices and ice cream. This is just one example of the humor and delight participants have taken in this highly unusual work.

The work has been recorded on the Soundspells Productions label by Atril Cinco, conducted by Limon, and the CD includes Kupferman's companion piece, *Flavors of the Stars* which is made up of eleven movements, each one a different "flavor" represented by a different instrument. Kupferman wrote it as a thank you to the performers, and it is as difficult and as challenging a work as the *Ice Cream Concerto*.

Sr. Limon obviously does the namesake Lemon on his guitar, followed with a vanilla cello, walnut English horn, peach marimba, chocolate electric bass, strawberry violin, cherry bass, coffee piano, orange guitar, mint flute, and pistachio percussion.

Why ice cream as a theme for a concerto? Kupferman says, "I just love ice cream. I eat it all the time."

A native of Manhattan, the seventy-one-year-old composer grew up during an era of outstanding ice cream pleasures: different varieties of ice cream cups, cream puffs like Charlotte Russe and, he confesses, a former weakness for banana splits and all those "soda fountain things." These days his passion for ice cream is as strong as ever, but "now I've discovered a chocolate-covered pop on a stick that only has 150 calories, so I can have one every day," he said. "Then, once a year, my wife makes a birthday cake of ice cream. On that day, it's an unrestricted feast of ice cream," he added.

RECORD-BREAKING EXCITEMENT WITH ICE CREAM

Interbake Dairy Ingredients created the *largest ice cream sandwich* on June 22, 1995. It measured three feet by eight feet by one foot high and weighed 830 pounds.*

Augusto, Ltd. of Kalisz, Poland, constructed the *largest ice cream bar* during the week of September 18, 1994, using chocolate, vanilla, and nut ice creams. It weighed 19,357 pounds.

Palm Dairies, Ltd. in Alberta, Canada made the world's *largest ice cream sundae* on July 24, 1988, weighing 54,914 pounds and 13 ounces. It included 44,689 pounds and 8 ounces of ice cream, 9,688 pounds and 2 ounces of syrup, and 537 pounds and 3 ounces of toppings.

Thomas Kemper Soda Company of Seattle made the world's *largest root beer float,* 2,100.5 gallons, on May 18, 1996. It wasn't just for show, either—nearly five hundred people drank it up.

The Guinness Book of World Records, 1997 ed.

THE FUTURE of ICE CREAM
and FROZEN DESSERTS

Frozen yogurt is not yogurt; it's a frozen dessert.
—David Bandler, professor of food science,
Cornell University

What's ahead? A general survey of reporters, manufacturers small and large, and key people in the dairy industry reveals that ice cream is definitely here to stay.

While I personally champion freshness, and lean toward either homemade or at least locally produced ice cream, the biggest share of the market is owned by large manufacturers, and will be in the future. The strength and power that huge corporations offer does mean excellent distribution channels, greater access to the prime grocery shelves, and the advertising that keeps the public informed of their products. Many of these large companies, however, make ice cream that may not even be delivered until six months after a batch is made. Through the miracles of chemistry, sophisticated freezing techniques, and improved refrigeration units in the retailer's store, ice cream is still "fresh tasting," despite its age. Time does not affect sales one iota.

There are changes afoot in the frozen dessert industry, though, and some are rather surprising.

Sales of low-fat and nonfat ice creams have declined slightly yet continually over the last five years, but sales for sorbets have jumped and prospects for growth are good. The reason? It seems consumers would rather have something nonfat and sweet (sorbets) but if they're going to have a treat like ice cream, they're going to buy "the real thing"—fat and all.

When frozen yogurt first hit the ice cream stores in the early 1970s, it was a sour milk dessert, reflecting the natural tang of the true yogurt culture. Several companies, Dannon and Beatrice among them, marketed a very icy and acidic frozen yogurt, which met with complete indifference or dislike at first.

Americans demanded a frozen yogurt that was sweeter and lower in fat. Edy's, allegedly the first to market frozen yogurt nationally, and its imitators followed with a greatly sweetened, greatly modified milk dessert that often had no live yogurt culture.

Despite a surge in popularity of frozen yogurts throughout the 1980s, sales dropped considerably during the 1990s, and the future does not look bright for this relative newcomer to the frozen dessert market. For a time, low and nonfat yogurts were the bulk of the frozen yogurts sold, but their sales have plummeted, most likely because they're notoriously high-calorie; in fact, some have hundreds of calories per scoop.

Some critics have requested that manufacturers put back the natural yogurt culture into frozen yogurt. They have encouraged a mandate for standardization, but that is a long way off, most industry watchers say. More important, the sweeter the product the more popular it is with the public, indicating that true yogurt culture will remain popular only in the "real thing," not in a dessert.

Offering new flavors on a regular basis has always been a good marketing ploy, as Howard Johnson, Baskin-Robbins, and Ben & Jerry's can attest. As the United States becomes even more a melting pot, the flavors of international cuisine also play a significant part in the frozen dessert market. It is now common to find mango, papaya, saputo, kiwi, and other "exotic" fruits like starfruit and rambutan in sorbets, ices, and ice creams.

Green tea was once the only tea product used in ice cream, but now you can find Earl Grey, Masala Chai, and other black tea flavors.

Coffee continues as a popular flavor in ice cream, sometimes mixed with other ingredients like chocolate, sometimes ranging in flavor from dark espresso to mild roast. Even Starbucks has gotten into the act, with some delicious coffee ice creams.

It is fascinating to know that not all flavors are popular everywhere; there remain decidedly regional tastes. For example, peanut butter, first created in Pennsylvania, is still a huge seller there yet almost unheard of west of the Mississippi. Coffee is a popular beverage; however, the smallest state in the union, Rhode Island, is the biggest consumer of coffee ice cream. Oregon, known for its incredible black raspberry, does not sell most of its berries in its own backyard. It is Pennsylvania which is the biggest purchaser of black raspberry sorbet and ice creams.

Vanilla is still number one, but one must recognize that it is also the basis for other flavors, desserts like milkshakes and sundaes, and for use in cake or pie à la mode because of its "neutral" flavor. Butter pecan, chocolate, and strawberry jockey for the other three top places. Their positions vary throughout the country but the changes are slight. Peach is one flavor everyone waxes nostalgic about, but its season is so limited, it never makes the top twenty list.

One certainty for the future is that the appetite for something new in the frozen dessert industry will remain strong. Consumers are always willing to try something new, in addition to still enjoying the desserts that conjure up the pleasures of childhood or other good times in their life. That relish for something familiar from childhood, plus niche marketing savvy, has helped the manufacturers of Popsicle, Fudgsicle, Klondike, Creamsicle, and Eskimo Pie, some selling treats more than seventy years old, remain steadfast fixtures of this dessert category.

The ice cream and frozen dessert industry has established excellent standards. Its dedication to innovation plays a vibrant role in answering consumers' needs for more sophisticated foods, more international flavors, more experimentation, and always, better quality in everything we eat or drink.

Whether you're committed to eating only homemade ice creams and frozen desserts to monitor quality and health, or want the convenience and excellence of fine frozen desserts at the supermarket, you have terrific choices. These will be available as long as you demand the best ingredients in everything you eat.

This is particularly important for ice cream and frozen desserts. They're the perfect finish of a great meal or a memorable day, a soothing treat when things are less than pleasing, or a way to chill off or chill out.

Always choose the best and enjoy it thoroughly.

After all, as we said at the beginning of this book, 'Life is short, eat dessert first.'

Making Ice Cream at Home

My advice to you is not to inquire why or whither but just enjoy your ice cream while it's on your plate—that's my philosophy.

—Thornton Wilder, *The Skin of Our Teeth*

Basic Techniques and Professional Tips

Most of the recipes we list in the book can be made with a couple of stainless steel bowls and a reliable freezer in a standard refrigerator. Because they're so readily available, fairly low-priced, and such a dream to use, consider one of the many ice cream machines at your appliance or kitchen store. Yes, appliance and hardware stores still offer the hand-cranked designs, and nostalgia is fun; but unless you have twenty or more neighborhood kids around who enjoy churning your ice cream for hours, you'll soon see the benefits of the electric ice cream machine.

The first and foremost rule in making any ice cream or frozen dessert, particularly those made with milk, is to clean, clean, clean your equipment. Even if you fastidiously clean the equipment before putting it away, always clean it immediately prior to using it again. Pour scalding hot water over both canisters and utensils, and thoroughly wipe them dry with a very clean cotton or linen towel. If you are using a canister type of machine, place the canister in the freezer at this point, or follow the manufacturer's directions.

Make sure that all your spoons and spatulas are scrupulously clean. This not only helps the recipe to work better, it helps to ward off any possible bacteria.

Freezing in bowls is easy, but use stainless steel bowls; preferably those that are large and have a flat bottom. Stainless steel is better than glass or ceramic because it goes from cold to hot and vice versa without any damage or breakage and will not react to acidic fruits as aluminum or copper can. Stainless steel is also preferable for utensils; a second choice would be wood spoons, which can tolerate temperature changes and won't be affected by acidic fruits.

When storing ice cream in the freezer, fill the container to the top or, if it is less than half full, cover it tightly with plastic wrap to keep air out. The objective is to avoid moisture that could form ice crystals and to avoid tainting the ice cream with other odors.

UH-OHS, OR WHY THE ICE CREAM DIDN'T COME OUT AS YOU PLANNED

Equipment isn't everything. You *can* make great ice cream with any method, whether you're using a fancy-schmancy electric machine or a hand-cranked wooden bucket freezer.

The keys to success are a good balance of ingredients, all of which are top quality; clean equipment and utensils; processing long enough and stirring well; and storing in a reliable freezer.

When it comes to the ingredients you use, fresh is the word. Farm-fresh eggs, fresh milk, fresh cream, fresh fruits, fresh, fresh, fresh. Fresh is important not just for taste, but for health. Eggs and milk are both vulnerable to bacteria, so if you have *any* doubt at all of the freshness of your ingredients, don't use them.

Your hands and everything you touch should be clean. When in doubt, wash again.

Because the coldness of the freezer unit varies so tremendously in home refrigerators, it is always a good idea to test your freezer unit before making a frozen dessert. If the temperature does not fluctuate, it can produce good frozen desserts. If the freezer temperature is too high, you may need to freeze your desserts longer than directed. Ideally, the freezer temperature should be between −4° and +2° F. Freezers whose temperatures go up and down versus those which are predictably a certain temperature are the worst problem-makers, and are unreliable for making frozen desserts.

Besides the quality of the ingredients and freezing them at a constant temperature, other factors go into producing good ice cream, particularly the type of stabilizers, and the amount of air and salt.

What if your ice cream comes out lumpy, bumpy, or syrupy? Below are listed some common problems found in both commercial and at-home frozen desserts. Commercial ice cream that has defrosted and been refrozen will certainly have a number of the problems listed below.

Generally, homemade ice cream problems center around freezing temperatures that are too high, failure to freeze long enough, or low-quality food ingredients. Here are some other suggestions for improvement:

Too Coarse. The texture is generally due to excess ice crystals. The most common reason is a freezer that freezes too slowly or has too much temperature fluctuation to allow the ice cream to harden properly. Other reasons are re-hardening soft ice cream, insufficient sugar, or too much air. In sorbets or ices, more frequent stirring, preferably with a chilled fork, is needed.

Gritty Texture. If the ice cream tastes like grit or sand in the mouth, it's most likely because the ice cream hardened too slowly, or the machine had too low a hardening temperature.

Watery Body. If the ice cream doesn't taste rich or melts too quickly, there is not enough of a stabilizer in the recipe, a frequent problem in noncustard ice creams. It could also be because there was too much air, a result of too high an overrun.

Too Crumbly. Actually, any crumbling is too much. This flaky texture is usually a result of a high overrun or too much air, but it could also mean too little stabilizer, especially in noncustard ice creams. Freezing at too low a temperature can also make the texture crumbly.

Spongy Texture.   Too much air or freezing the cream into too soft a mixture usually results in this unappealing spongy texture. A close relative, **gummy texture**, is more like Silly Putty. It is caused by too little air or too much stabilizer.

Melting Problems.   Overfreezing, inaccurate salt balance, or milk protein instability usually results in a **globby texture**. Smooth, rich ice cream should melt evenly and slowly.

Failure to Melt.   If it doesn't seem to melt at all it has too much fat, too many stabilizers, or was frozen at too low a temperature. One can leave a brick of poor-grade ice cream out of its box overnight, and it will barely melt. This is not a good thing. It is one more reason to buy the best, or to make your own.

> *Do you think that God made good things only for fools?*
> —Descartes, on being asked about his
> fondness for sweet things

ICE CREAM MACHINES

Following the manufacturer's directions is the key to getting the best product from any commercial freezer. Below are some general guidelines.

Crank Type

Sentiment aside, the crank-type bucket freezer still produces the most "udderly delicious" ice cream you'll ever taste. No lesser authorities than Irma E. Rombauer and Marion Rombauer Becker, authors of the American cookbook classic *The Joy of Cooking*, swear by the venerable White Mountain Freezer as the machine of choice for the creamiest ice cream. More than one hundred years old, White Mountain is still going strong under its new parent company, The Rival Company.

The bucket freezer, sometimes referred to as a crank freezer or churn freezer, is usually made of pine wood, which is soaked prior to each use to prevent leaks. The bucket holds a smaller canister or container that fits securely inside.

The canister is fitted with a stationary paddle called a dasher with wood blades that scrape the sides of the canister as it turns. It is turned or rotated by hand with a crank, although some old-fashioned-looking bucket freezers actually have electric motors, combining technology with nostalgia for greater ease of operation.

To make ice cream, the freezer requires a mixture of three-fourths crushed ice and one-fourth rock salt. Some bucket freezers may use ice cubes and ordinary table salt. Because the texture of ice cream depends upon the speed of the processing, a slower speed will produce a smoother texture and a faster speed will produce a creamier texture. Salt has an effect, too. Increased salt will shorten the freezing time and give an icier texture; less salt will lengthen the freezing time and give a finer, smoother texture.

ICE CREAM MOMENT

Sally Champe, interior designer, Sausalito, California

When I was a very little girl during the forties, Sunday afternoons were often spent playing with my cousins in the backyard of my grandfather's house in Burbank, California. His property was full of fruit trees—peach, lemon, apricot. Climbing the gnarly, old, beautiful apricot tree, redolent with the sweet aroma of ripe apricots, we would look over each one, pick only the best, blemish-free fruit, and gently carry them as we wended our way down the tree (or more often, simply jumped off).

We offered these beautiful golden-red apricots, warmed from the sun, to our grandfather to place with the thick rich milk in his old-timey crank ice cream freezer. The process of making home-made ice cream was long and arduous, and only the men operated the machine, each taking ten-minute turns at the crank.

The men, my grandfather's sons and sons-in-law, were newly home from the War, still wearing their uniforms, which made them, to our child eyes, gallant, handsome, and very brave. Reflecting back, I'm sure they never discussed the real stories of their war experiences, probably not even with their wives, and certainly not with us, but they did talk about some funny things they saw or did or the incorrigibles among their troops.

Our favorite story was the ironic meeting of two of my uncles, brothers, one of whom was stationed in the Pacific Theater, the other sent to Europe. Imagine their astonishment to find themselves side by side, totally by chance, during the Invasion of Normandy.

While the men told their tales, continuously cranking the ice cream machine, the women cooked the Sunday dinner that would once again join our family together, grateful that all had returned to us safe and sound. For dessert there was, of course, the apricot ice cream, barely a quart of it despite all the hard work, but oh so good. Creamy, cold, smooth, with that inexplicably delicate perfume of apricots.

Pre-Chilled Canister Units

Some of these machines are not much more than toys. They often produce an uneven product, but if you freeze the canister well and your refrigerator's freezer is reliable, then the end result will usually be good.

The Donvier is typical of this style of freezer. It does sorbets very well. Named for the Japanese firm that invented it, this machine uses a pre-chilled canister freezer with a sealed, hollow metal canister filled with a coolant instead of ice or rock salt. The canister is frozen for twenty-four to forty-eight hours prior to making ice cream and then filled with a chilled ice cream or sorbet mixture. It has crank and dasher equipment similar to that of the bucket freezer, and is hand cranked, but one only has to crank about twelve to eighteen minutes. It produces a dense, creamy ice cream.

The canister-type of freezer is very popular because it's so easy to operate, but it isn't foolproof. The most important things to remember are never to cover it with anything when it is in the freezer and to make sure lid and ring are spotlessly dry before using.

Care must be taken to make sure the cylinder is sufficiently frozen, but it will not be if:

- you open and close the door too often, anxious to taste the final result;
- containers of food block the cold air vent at the back of the freezer;
- the container was not allowed to freeze long enough (seven hours or overnight is suggested) or was allowed to come to room temperature;
- the container was placed upside down or on its side (if you have too much food in your freezer, make ice cream later, or eat those frozen peas already!); or,
- the ingredients were warmer than the cylinder; ergo, the colder your ingredients, the better they will freeze.

Electric Units

These are no-brainers, no effort, no work, but you pay for the privilege to pour, turn on, and wait. The price range is amazing, from $40 to more than $400. Unless you're going to make frozen desserts daily, however, opt for the lower-priced items. Based on the same principles as the hand cranked units, they produce an incredibly smooth, extra dense sorbet or ice cream.

The Waring is a good middle-of-the-road machine, with models from $40 to $90. The Simac II Gelatiaio is big, and exceptionally well-built, and makes terrific ice cream. It is the machine of choice for many restaurants. If I had money to burn, I'd buy the Simac, but even with gourmet ice cream costing $3 a pint, one would have to make 133 homemade pints to get one's money back, at that high price tag. If you're a pint-a-day person, this might figure out to be a bargain, and you'll get fabulous ice cream to boot. Gelato Modo and Vilantonio are two other fine Italian ice cream machines that are mentioned frequently by restaurateurs.

Pot Freezer

This is the method used by George Washington which he adapted from observing ice cream made in France.

ACCESSORIES

Agnes Marshall of London did more to champion molded desserts than anyone else in the early twentieth century. Her shop, which served as both cooking school and retail store, had at one time more than two thousand different shapes and sizes of molds for creating bombes, vegetable and fruit terrines, and ices.

Highly collectible, ice cream molds were generally made of pewter, although some of the more expensive ones were made of copper. Should you discover tin or tin-lined copper molds in antique stores, use them only for decorations, as worn tin is potentially poisonous.

Although pewter is considered by some people to be unhealthful because of its high lead content, it remains the most popular material for ice cream molds. Some experts believe it is the use of cold temperature versus hot that makes pewter work well and be safe.

Aluminum copies of old lead molds are okay to use, but line them with wax paper to prevent the metallic taste that aluminum sometimes gives off.

None of these cautions should stop you from buying the molds if you're in the mood to collect; they are pretty and, quite often, very well made. Some molds had little legs so that they could stand on the table. The hinged top would open and the chef could then unmold his creation with ease.

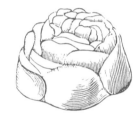

Ice Cream Molds

Edible servers were quite the rage in the early 1900s, and these molds were also used to create bowls or forms made like flowers or animals in ice that set off the vegetable or fruited sorbet nicely. The server melted slowly to keep the dessert chilled, and it was truly ecologically sound.

Then, as now, creative cooks have used the peel of fruits to create containers in which to serve their desserts. It's a relatively simple thing to do and is quite dramatic. Fruits like oranges or grapefruits are ideal and can be used both for desserts made of the fruit or for contrasting flavors. Simply slice off the top of the orange, for example, hollow out the fruit, and set the shelled fruit aside. Make the sorbet or ice cream as planned, return the hollowed-out peel to a plate, stuff it with the dessert, replace the top you sliced off as a "cap," and there you have it. Decorate the plate with a ribbon of complimentary syrup or add a few cookies and you have a charming way to serve your frozen dessert.

ICE CREAM CONE

Cones are readily available, but nothing tastes so fresh and crisp as a wafer shell you make yourself. It does help, of course, to have professional equipment like a pizelle or electric ice-cream cone maker, but an electric waffle iron serves quite well. This recipe allows you to make cones with pointed ends and open tops for the ice cream, but probably nothing smaller or tighter.

    1 cup sugar
    ⅓ cup sweet butter, allowed to rest at room temperature
    4 egg whites
    1¼ cups sifted all-purpose flour
    1 teaspoon cornstarch or arrowroot powder

Preheat oven to 375° F and grease baking sheets if not using the nonstick kind. Sift sugar into a bowl and rub in butter (hands are best!) until you have a crumbly mix. Add egg whites one at a time, and beat smoothly with hand-held mixer or large spoon until smooth. In a separate bowl, combine flour and corn-starch, and sift together in a bowl. Fold in sugar-butter mixture until all is smooth.

Pour a large spoonful at a time on the cookie sheet, about 4 inches in diam-eter. They do not spread much so they can be placed fairly close to one another. Bake for about six minutes or until lightly brown, preferably in the middle of the oven. Remove immediately and shape into a cone, using a narrow spatula to fold over the edges.

To use an electric waffle griddle, follow the manufacturer's directions. If it is a nonstick type, simply pour mixture in the size you want it (about 4 inches). If you must oil the griddle, use a canola or other bland-tasting oil. Butter tends to make the cones burn.

Whether you make cones on a cookie sheet or in a griddle, they're best eaten the day you make them. If you're feeling very ambitious, you can coat them with chocolate by dipping them into melted chocolate, and cooling them on waxed paper.

SODA FOUNTAIN DESSERTS

For soda fountain desserts, nothing beats glass bowls and tumblers to show off the color and drama of sundaes, sodas, and milk shakes. Many large drugstores still sell such glassware at reasonable prices.

Finding the metal dishes are more of an effort, but many restaurant supply stores carry them, and some specialty catalog companies offer them, including Williams-Sonoma. Thrift stores, flea markets, and other secondhand shops are always good sources for the real thing, and catalogs and stores often carry reproductions of these old-time soda fountain accessories.

When serving frozen desserts at home, it's critical to have a good-quality spade or scoop. There are hundreds of styles and shapes. I prefer the Italian style with the black rubber handle and smooth spadelike scoop. The rubber helps my grip and is good for any size hand, and the spade style helps scoop out even the hardest ice cream. It's really a matter of personal taste. Some people like the spring mechanism of a bowl scoop because it helps release the scoop without having to resort to another spoon or, heavens, one's fingers.

You can find scoops everywhere from the local supermarket to hardware stores, to kitchen and cookery shops. To test, ask how the handle feels in your hand, whether the weight is even or "scoop-heavy" and if it does or does not have a spring mechanism to release the ice cream. Black or white goes with everything, but some scoops come in dramatic colors that are fun to have around.

ICE CREAM MOMENT

Marie Henry, San Rafael, California

My only foray into a life of crime involved ice cream. Years ago, when my brother and his wife went on vacation, I was bringing in their mail when I noticed a birthday postcard from Farrell's Ice Cream Parlor addressed to my sister-in-law Marcia. Since I knew she wouldn't be back in time to redeem it, and, after all, ice cream was one of my major passions in life, I wasn't about to let a free ice cream sundae go unclaimed.

I put on my innocent face as I opened the door to Farrell's, walked up to the counter, and handed over the illicit postcard, mumbling, "Hi, I got this in the mail."

"Take a seat," the kid at the counter said, "It'll be ready in a few minutes."

I sat down on the uncomfortably hard little round wooden seat of the dainty-looking wrought iron chair, and waited to be called up to get my ice cream sundae. Imagine my horror when, out from the kitchen, came six fresh-faced young kids singing a rousing version (complete with marching band drum—or did I only dream that part?) of "Happy Birthday, Dear Marcia," as they ceremoniously presented me with a little ice cream sundae meant for somebody else.

I almost slid out of my chair, wishing I could hide under the table. The waiters stood applauding "my" natal day, and probably thought I was just shy about the attention I was getting. Hardly. My mortification had nothing to do with shyness. It was sheer guilt. I always thought I'd do anything for a free ice cream . . . but after that experience, I wasn't so sure anymore.

(Note: Marie Henry finally told her sister-in-law
about her "ice cream crime" twenty years later.)

Recipes

There was a young lady of Michigan,
To see her I never could wish again.
She would eat of ice cream
Till with pain she would scream,
Then order another big dish again.
—Jarrolds' *Complete Limerick Book*, 1924

Classics

*Ice cream is eaten with a spoon, but when served as a part of
Baked Alaska or with cake, it is eaten with a dessert fork and spoon.*
—*The Amy Vanderbilt Complete Book of Etiquette Entirely Rewritten
and Updated*, by Nancy Dunnan and Nancy Tuckerman,
Doubleday

Basic Sugar Syrup

Sweeteners of all kinds can and have been used to make frozen ices or ice creams, including corn or malted syrups, beet, milk, or corn sugars, sucrose, and fructose.

The simplest is still the best: white cane sugar and good quality water. This combination produces a clear, clean, unfettered sweetener that accommodates your favorite flavorings and does not negatively affect either the texture or the overall quality of the ice cream. The following proportion gives a nice sweet taste; you can, however, increase or decrease the sugar to your preference. Generally, a one-to-one ratio is best, but this includes just a dash more sugar.

$1^3/_8$ cup sugar
$1^1/_4$ cup spring water, previously heated to a boil and cooled slightly

Dissolve sugar in the hot water. Use this mixture to experiment with your own recipes. It's particularly good in making fruit sorbets.

Basic Vanilla

This traditional recipe contains no eggs, yet makes a very rich, satisfying recipe. Vanilla beans are pricey, but worth every penny.

6 cups light cream
$1^1/_4$ cups granulated sugar

$^1/_8$ teaspoon salt
2 vanilla beans, split

In a double boiler, combine 3 cups of cream with the sugar, salt, and the vanilla beans. Stir constantly while cooking for ten minutes. Remove vanilla beans. Scrape the vanilla bean pulp and seeds from the pods and put back into the cream mixture. Allow to cool, add the remaining three cups of cream, and mix well. Put into ice cream freezer container and freeze according to manufacturer's directions. *Serves four.*

I think Ben & Jerry's Vanilla is great, and the quart is priced the same as the pint; such a deal. Most premium vanillas are great, but I found some of the major brands too dry.

BASIC CHOCOLATE

5 tablespoons cocoa powder (Van Houten's, which is Dutch, or Feodora, which is German; they're simply fabulous. Available at Trader Joe's and other specialty markets.)

$\frac{1}{2}$ cup sugar

$1\frac{1}{2}$ cups whole milk

5 ounces chopped semi-sweet European chocolate

3 egg yolks

1 teaspoon pure natural vanilla extract

$\frac{1}{4}$ cup sugar syrup (made from spring water and sugar and boiled to a syrup)

1 cup heavy whipping cream

Combine the cocoa and half the sugar and pour in enough milk to form a thin paste. Using a double boiler for this recipe, heat water in the bottom part on a separate burner while you bring the remainder of the milk to a boil, then slowly pour the milk into the paste, stirring constantly. Put the mixture back into the top part of the double boiler; place it atop the now-boiling water in the bottom part of the double boiler. Cook very gently for about 5 to 8 minutes or until all the powdery cocoa is cooked out; not a speck of cocoa dust should remain. Remove from heat and stir in the chopped chocolate until smooth, and set aside.

In a separate bowl, beat the egg yolks together with the remaining sugar until it is a pale creamy yellow. Pour the sugar-egg mixture into the chocolate mixture, this time beating hard to incorporate the two items. Warm again in the top of the double boiler, stirring until the temperature reaches 185° F, which is under boiling; do not allow it to boil. Remove from heat again and add vanilla extract. Cool the mixture in a bath of cold water. Cover and chill in the refrigerator about 2 hours. Beat in the whipping cream into the chocolate mixture and pour all into an ice cream maker, following the manufacturer's directions. Freeze again for about 2 more hours. *Serves six regular people and three chocoholics.*

STORE-BOUGHT

I have rarely bought a chocolate ice cream I didn't like, but my favorite (this week) is not an ice cream but the chocolate sorbet from Häagen-Dazs; it's intense, pure chocolate. Who needs anything more? If you love dark chocolate candy, this is a chilly version. If you love milk chocolate candy, consider chocolate ice creams from Portofino, Ciao Bella Gelato, and good old Baskin-Robbins.

BASIC STRAWBERRY

The strawberry is one fruit that should be used in season, to capture its heady sweetness. As with our vanilla recipe, we use a vanilla bean versus a vanilla extract. There simply is nothing more exquisite or more worth the price. This is not a low-fat dessert, but since it makes two quarts, one can be satisfied with a spoon at a time over a respectable length of time. It's worth every calorie. If you have a small ice cream maker, you might have to make this in two batches or halve the recipe.

1 ½ cups heavy cream
½ cup milk
1 vanilla bean, split and scraped
4 egg yolks
6 pints of fresh summer strawberries, picked over, destemmed and cleaned

1 ¾ cups sugar
¼ cup fresh lemon juice
Strawberries for garnish
Chocolate cookies

Set a stainless steel bowl over a larger bowl of ice and set aside. Combine the heavy cream, milk, and scraped vanilla bean in a saucepan and bring mixture to a boil. Cover pan and let steep about 15 minutes with the heat turned completely off.

Beat egg yolks in a large bowl and gradually add ¼ cup sugar until mixture is a creamy yellow. Warm the vanilla cream mixture and pour it over the egg yolks, stirring constantly to avoid curdling. Pour back into the saucepan and heat over a small flame until thick enough to coat a wooden spoon.

Pour mixture back into the stainless bowl set over a bowl of ice, and cool. Strain mixture through a sieve to remove the flecks of the vanilla bean and set aside.

Puree enough strawberries in a blender or food processor to have six cups. Add 1 ½ cups of sugar plus the lemon juice and process only until combined. If too tart, add 1 or 2 more tablespoons of sugar. Combine fruit puree with the vanilla cream into an ice cream maker and follow the manufacturer's instructions.

Serve with garnishes of fresh strawberries or chocolate cookies. Makes about two quarts. *Serves about sixteen.*

STORE-BOUGHT
Bud's of San Francisco has a strawberry ice cream that really tastes like strawberries and cream. Dolley Madison would have loved it. Bud's is primarily distributed in the West. Coleman's in Pennsylvania comes close.

BUTTER PECAN

STORE-BOUGHT

Yes, Virginia, I did meet an ice cream I didn't like, and this is it—too sweet for my taste. In the spirit of why Baskin-Robbins has thirty-one flavors, however, enjoy. Where to find the best? My advice, buy local, buy fresh. Considering that pecans grow best in Georgia and Texas, Edy's and other local vendors in those states are good selections.

CATHY BROWN'S PEACH ICE CREAM

An apple is an excellent thing—till you have tried a peach.
—George du Maurier, *Trilby*

My friend Cathy Brown, a native of Florida, is a terrific cook who can entertain two or a hundred with equal aplomb. As for ice cream, she says, "True Southerners do not consume store-bought ice cream. They crank it themselves, since there is so little else to do, and it's a way to chat and pass the time. Recipes are passed down through the generations, and no self-respecting Southern lady would be without her favorite homemade sherbet recipe, which is just the ticket to cut through all the hog jowls and fried chicken which precede its service. Now, in these parts, homemade peach ice cream reigns supreme. I offer you my own family recipe."

10 cups of ripe peaches, peeled, and chopped (about six pounds) (This recipe needs no sugar; if the peaches aren't sweet and juicy, just don't bother with them. Adding additional sugar isn't going to help.)

4 cups heavy cream
2 teaspoons of pure vanilla extract
1 tablespoon ground ginger

Put half the peaches in a large mixing bowl. Puree the rest of the peaches in a food processor until mushy, then add to the bowl of chopped peaches. Add the cream, vanilla, and ginger and mix thoroughly. Place in a hand-cranked freezer and churn until cold and thick. Place in the freezer for an hour or more. Fabulous. *Serves six.*

STORE-BOUGHT

There is no such thing as great store-bought peach ice cream. Some local vendors do come close, but I've never had one. This is definitely a flavor to make at home. Believe me, it's worth it.

ICE CREAM MOMENT

Miss Dona, Sausalito, California

During the hot, humid, sticky-icky summers of my girlhood in Brooklyn, my idea of the perfect summer meal was to go to the Carvel's (we wouldn't just go anywhere, it *had* to be Carvel's) and pick up four pints of ice cream, one each for my dad, my brother, my mom, and me. We "girls" always had chocolate, of course, and the "boys" always had strawberry. We grew up with the rationalization that ice cream in the summer was one of the four food groups. I still think it's a great idea for a summer meal, but today I eat either coffee frozen yogurt with *real* chocolate syrup or chocolate sorbet, both by Häagen-Dazs.

TEA AND COFFEE

Because I write frequently about tea and coffee, I couldn't resist including a few recipes made with my favorite brews. You'll find tea and coffee selections in the granita section as well.

So many great coffee ice creams are in your grocer's freezer, but the new selections from Starbucks Coffee Company, a joint venture with Dreyer's Grand Ice Cream, Inc., really are good, most likely because they're made with great coffee. The Dark Roast Espresso with Chocolate is a combination of two superb food groups, chocolate and coffee. For a low-fat choice, Healthy Choice's Cappuccino Chocolate Chunk is mighty fine, and Häagen-Dazs's low-fat Coffee Chocolate Swirl is so rich with chocolate that you won't miss the fat.

For coffee, freshly brewed is best; the richer and darker the roast the better. I like espresso in particular for ice creams, but experiment until you get the coffee taste you like best. Mixing in some finely crushed coffee beans is the pièce de résistance for many ardent coffee lovers.

Thanks to great vendors, coffee choices are legion. Choose a coffee slightly stronger than you usually have for drinking so that the intensity of the cold will not drown out the flavor. For example, a dark Italian or French roasted bean or a rich coffee bean ground for espresso would be just right.

Coffee extracts and instant coffees are second choices, and are obviously convenient.

Coffee liqueurs add a nice touch, but do not add more liqueur than the recipes call for since alcohol of any type will affect the freezing process and interfere with creating a smooth-textured dessert. If you would like to use a coffee-flavored liqueur like Kahlua, Tia Maria, or Benedictine, reduce the sugar, because the liqueur itself is a concentrated sweet taste. For example, if you use $1\frac{1}{2}$ tablespoons of liqueur, reduce the sugar by about $\frac{1}{4}$ cup or more to your taste.

Tea in ice cream is a fairly new phenomenon except for green tea but many ice cream makers aim to change that by adding Masala Chai flavoring, Earl Grey, Black Currant, Thai or Ginger Tea to a pure vanilla base.

As with coffee, using fine teas will give you fine ice cream. The key to extracting the best flavor without unwanted astringency or bitterness is to use cool spring water and brew slowly. If using teas for a milk-based dessert, you can either infuse the tea in cool spring water for up to 4 hours (do not boil the water) or infuse it in milk overnight or for up to 8 hours. Loose-leaf teas always give a better flavor. Strain the leaves before using the liquid. Tea is the ultimate recycled food—just use the leaves for your plants or compost and back to nature it goes.

EARL GREY ICE CREAM

⅔ cup very strong Earl Grey tea, infused in cool water and steeped for at least ½ hour. This will make a strong brew without bitterness.
⅔ cup light cream

⅔ cup cream, whipped
1 long strip of lemon peel, about 5 inches, pith removed
3 egg yolks
½ cup sugar
3 vanilla wafer cookies

In a heavy-bottomed saucepan, put the tea, light cream, and lemon peel in together and bring to just below the simmering point. In a bowl, beat the egg yolks and sugar together until thick and whisk in the hot liquid, pouring it in slowly. Remove the lemon peel and set peel aside.

In another pan, pour in the mixture and cook over low heat, stirring constantly until the custard thickens. Return the lemon peel to the pan and stir occasionally. Leave to cool. Remove lemon peel again, and pour the mixture into a container. Cover and freeze until almost firm, about 3 hours. Turn into a bowl, beat, and then fold in the whipped cream.

Return the mixture to the container. Cover and freeze until firm, about 6 hours. Scoop out into small bowls and garnish with sprinkles of lemon zest. Serve with a vanilla wafer cookie. *Makes three to four small servings.*

STORE-BOUGHT

An excellent commercial Earl Grey ice cream is actually a gelato, from Ciao Bella, available in most upscale markets. Its Chai, with the quirky ginger, vanilla, and pumpkin spice flavors, is also another winner.

GREEN TEA ICE CREAM

This is a rich, custard version of this classic Japanese dish. Use a mild green tea, brewed slowly from loose leaves for about $1/2$ hour with *cold water*, about 8 ounces of water to one large heaping tablespoon of a spiderleg or gyokuro. The cold water is important for extracting the flavor without the typical astringency of green tea made with water that is too hot (a definite no-no!).

1 8-ounce cup of strong green tea, preferably spiderleg or gyokuro	2 cups whipping cream
	2 teaspoons vanilla extract
5 egg yolks	$1/2$ teaspoon freshly grated orange zest
1 cup sugar	
1 cup half and half	$1/8$ teaspoon freshly ground nutmeg

Chill a large bowl in the refrigerator for whipping the cream. Put the tea leaves in a glass measuring cup and fill with spring water. Allow the tea to steep at room temperature while you start preparing the other ingredients.

In a saucepan, whisk together the egg yolks until creamy yellow. Whisk in the sugar slowly, a little at a time. Set aside.

In a second saucepan, combine the half and half with one cup of the whipping cream, and, stirring gently with a wooden spoon, heat just until tiny bubbles form around the edge. Lower the temperature and cook about ten more minutes, continuing to stir. Very slowly, stir this hot mixture into the egg yolks. (If you pour it in too fast, the hot mixture will curdle the egg yolks.) Continue cooking over low heat, stirring constantly until the mixture coats the spoon. Remove from heat. Stir in the vanilla.

Allow to cool slightly, then pour the entire mixture into a large glass bowl and cover with plastic wrap. Chill in the refrigerator about 4 hours. Strain the tea leaves and chill the tea liquor in the refrigerator, well-covered.

In the chilled bowl, beat the remaining cup of whipping cream until peaks form. Stir in the tea liquor, orange zest, and grated nutmeg, and fold gently into the chilled mixture. Pour your completely mixed ingredients into your electric ice cream freezer, following its directions. If it's too pale a color, you could add a couple drops of green food coloring, or serve it in bowls that are hunter green for color effect. *Serves ten.*

STORE-BOUGHT

I think there is nothing finer than Double Rainbow's Green Tea ice cream. Perfection.

If they like it, it serves four; otherwise, six.
—Elsie Zussman

ESPRESSO ICE CREAM

If I had my druthers, all coffee would be espresso; it's simply the distillation of all that is grand about coffee; thick, rich, and just a few sips of perfection.

    4 eggs, separated
 $^1/_3$ cup sugar
    3 tablespoons finely-ground espresso
    2 cups heavy cream, whipped to show peaks
      Cocoa powder

Whip egg yolks together with the sugar until the mixture is a pale, creamy yellow. Stir in the espresso and then gently fold in the whipped cream.

In a separate bowl (copper is best, but a scrupulously cleaned glass bowl will do), beat egg whites until soft peaks form. Stir in about one-fourth of the egg whites into the egg and sugar mixture, then gently fold in the remaining whites in a few quick stirrings. Pour into a container and cover tightly. Freeze for about 2 hours. Take it out and whip again and return to the freezer for another 2 hours. Serve in bright white bowls, and dust the ice cream with cocoa powder. *Serves four.*

STORE-BOUGHT

Ciao Bella wins again with its Espresso Gelato; this is "the One" for people who love potent coffee flavor. If they love coffee but not necessarily espresso, serve them Häagen-Dazs's Coffee or any of the selections from Starbucks; now, that's real coffee.

CHOCOLATE COFFEE ICE CREAM

This is a great recipe to try if you do not have a regular ice cream freezer. It takes two sessions of freezing, so plan ahead, but rest assured that the combination of chocolate and coffee with the tang of cherries is an incredible taste sensation. Use the best chocolate syrup you can buy; it really makes the difference. I love Fran's Chocolates, Ltd. of Seattle. Sinful. Sensational. Satisfying.

2 cups freshly brewed, double-strength espresso (Kenya AA, if possible)	1 teaspoon pure vanilla extract
$^1/_4$ cup granulated sugar	$^2/_3$ cup cherries, well drained (Clearbrook Red Tart Michigan variety is superb.)
2 cups whipping cream	$^2/_3$ cup chopped walnuts
1 $^1/_3$ cups sweetened condensed milk	
16 ounces Fran's Gold Bar chocolate syrup	

Combine the coffee and sugar together in a bowl and stir until the sugar is completely dissolved. Cover the bowl and chill in the refrigerator. While it is chilling, mix together the whipping cream, condensed milk, chocolate syrup, and vanilla extract at low to medium speed in an electric mixer until soft peaks form. Remove the chilled coffee mixture and stir it into the whipped cream mixture. Transfer the new mixture into a large pan (9 by 13 inches) and freeze, covered, for up to 8 hours or overnight. Remove from freezer and let stand for about 12 to 15 minutes until slightly softened, and put into a large bowl. Beat again at low speed until almost smooth. Stir in the cherries and chopped walnuts. Wash pan thoroughly and dry well. Put the cherry- and walnut-studded mixture back into the pan and freeze another 8 hours or overnight. *Serves about sixteen.*

STORE-BOUGHT

Healthy Choice's Cappuccino Mocha Fudge is low in fat but high in flavor, and Häagen-Dazs's Low-Fat Coffee Fudge is another surprising low-fat combo. If calories are not an issue, try any of the new Starbucks coffee ice creams. If you're in Rhode Island (the largest consumer of coffee ice cream in the country) everywhere you find local creameries you will find paradise.

> *A sallow waiter brings me beans and pork . . .*
> *Outside there's fury in the firmament*
> *Ice-cream of course, will follow; and*
> *I'm content. O Babylon! O Cathay! O New York!*
> —Siegfried Sassoon, "Storm on Fifth Avenue"

ICE CREAMS LIKE CHEFS MAKE

Commercial fruit purees are fast becoming a staple in the sophisticated restaurant kitchen, and soon will be available in your gourmet grocer's freezer. These precooked, sieved, and blended products offer consistent quality in both texture and flavor and ease of preparation. One of the best is The Perfect Purée of Napa Valley, whose founder, Terry Hayward, shares these spectacular ice cream recipes.

CASSIS ICE CREAM

3 cups light cream
3 cups heavy cream
2 cups Perfect Purée*
    Classic Cassis (Black Currant)
    thawed

2 cups granulated sugar
Raspberries
Boysenberries

In a large bowl, stir together all the ingredients until well blended. Pour into an ice cream maker and freeze according to manufacturer's directions. This is a richly flavored ice cream, and the piquant tartness of fresh raspberries or boysenberries is just the right touch. *Serves eight.*

CRIMSON CRANBERRY ICE CREAM

This is an ideal treat for the holidays, and an unusually refreshing dessert for any season.

3 cups light cream
3 cups heavy cream
2 cups Perfect Purée Holiday
    Cranberry, thawed

1 1/2 cups granulated sugar
Fresh berries or cherries

*If Perfect Purée products are not yet available in your area, you can substitute frozen fruits; taste and adjust for sweetness.

In a large bowl, stir together all the ingredients until well blended and pour into an ice cream maker. Freeze according to manufacturer's directions. For the holiday, what better garnish than peppermint candy or a candy cane? Depending on the season, bing cherries or fresh berries are just the right touch. *Serves eight.*

Too much of a good thing is wonderful.
—Mae West

KULFI

Writing about tea has given me the opportunity to try many exotic dishes from around the world, particularly Sri Lankan, Chinese, Japanese, and Indian cuisine. Indian ice cream is some of the richest, most sensuous in the world. Here is our version of this confection. You'll soon see what we mean by rich and sensuous.

1 ¹/₂ cups milk	¹/₄ teaspoon pure almond extract
1 cup cream	1 tablespoon rosewater
2 eggs plus 2 egg yolks	¹/₄ cup whipping cream
¹/₂ cup sugar	2 tablespoons toasted sliced
¹/₃ cup ground toasted almonds	almonds, for garnish

Bring milk and cream slowly to boiling in a heavy-bottomed saucepan. Beat together eggs, egg yolks, and sugar in a bowl until well blended. Gradually stir in the hot cream and milk mixture. Pour back into the saucepan and cook gently over low heat, stirring constantly until the consistency of a thick custard. *Do not boil.*

Remove from heat and allow to cool, about 30 minutes. Stir ground almonds, almond extract, and rosewater into the custard mixture and pour all into a container. Cover and chill in the refrigerator for at least 30 minutes, then freeze until slushy, about 2 hours.

Whip the whipping cream in a bowl until soft peaks form. Beat the custard mixture well. Gently fold the whipping cream into the custard mixture. Pour back into the cover and freeze until firm, about 12 hours or overnight. About $\frac{1}{2}$ hour before serving, remove the container from the freezer and put into the refrigerator. Spoon into small bowls and garnish with toasted sliced almonds. *Serves four.*

VARIATION

Pistachios can be substituted for the almonds. The recipe remains the same, except for the deletion of almond extract. It's time-consuming to shell and then peel off the skins of the nuts, but if you love pistachios, you'll love Pistachio Kulfi and think the effort greatly worth the final result.

STORE-BOUGHT

Reena's, a popular brand name of kulfi available in most Indian grocers, offers ice cream bars or pints of papaya; salupo, a Chinese fruit that is also grown in India; cashew and raisin; pistachio; saffron, and almond. Worth the trip to wherever the grocer is; not for the cholesterol-phobic.

GARLIC ICE CREAM

Believe it or not, chocolate and garlic go together rather well, according to the contributor of this recipe, poet Mara Teitel. She uses a "generic" vanilla ice cream base. Toward the end of processing the ice cream, add fudge swirl to jazz it up. You could also use a basic chocolate ice cream base. This recipe is definitely one to astonish guests.

10 cloves fresh garlic
$\frac{1}{2}$ cup maple syrup
2 cups heavy cream
2 cups light cream

1 cup sugar
1 $\frac{1}{2}$ teaspoons pure vanilla extract
$\frac{1}{8}$ teaspoon salt

Drop garlic cloves into a saucepan of boiling water and cook for about 5 minutes, till tender. Peel and chop garlic and soak it in the maple syrup for 20 minutes, then drain. Pour cream into a bowl and add sugar, vanilla, and salt, and stir with a wooden spoon until the sugar dissolves. Add drained garlic to the mixture and stir. Place mixture into your ice cream canister and follow manufacturer's directions. *Serves six.*

SHERBETS

*In the whole array of terms used in the culinary art, there are
few of larger application or more uncertain meaning than the
word sherbet.*

—*Ices Plain and Fancy,* by Fred T. Vine,
aka Compton Dene, 1890

Sherbets are similar to sorbets, but usually contain milk or yogurt, although some also contain gelatin to help the ingredients congeal. They're ideal for making with fruits. The fruit is best cooked until tender with sweeteners, cooled, then pureed with milk and sugar syrup. The following recipes, however, need no cooking. Use stainless steel bowls and utensils or wooden spoons.

ORANGE SHERBET

This is a breeze to make.

2 cups milk

2 cups fresh orange juice
(To use orange rinds as a
serving container, cut
oranges in half with serrated
knife. Set aside rinds after
juicing.)

2 tablespoons fresh lemon juice

$^3/_4$ cup sugar syrup (see page 86)

$^1/_2$ teaspoon orange extract
or $^1/_4$ teaspoon orange
or rose water

6 chocolate wafer cookies

In a large bowl, mix all the ingredients together and pour into an ice cream freezer container and follow the manufacturer's directions for freezing. To serve, scoop out orange sherbet and tamp down into orange rinds. If they do not sit perfectly, make a small slice at the bottom to help them rest evenly on the plate. Garnish with orange segments and serve with chocolate wafer cookies. *Serves about six.*

LEMON SHERBET

1 $^1/_3$ cup sugar

$^1/_4$ teaspoon salt

1 quart of whole milk

1 $^1/_3$ cups fresh lemon juice
(about 8 lemons)

1 $^1/_3$ tablespoons grated lemon
zest (make sure there is no
white pith)

8 sprigs of mint

Mix together the sugar, salt, and milk until the sugar is dissolved. Stirring constantly, add the lemon juice and zest very slowly to avoid curdling the milk. Put into your ice cream maker, following the directions. Makes a lovely, refreshing sherbet. Garnish with a sprig of mint. *Serves eight generously.*

LIME SHERBET PUNCH

What would a holiday party, summer bridal shower, or Southern ladies' lunch be without lime sherbet punch? This was the first "recipe" I ever learned for party food, and I must admit, it's still refreshing and delicious, and so pretty. You'll need one large punch bowl and a dozen cups, plus a ladle for serving.

  2 **chilled quarts of ginger ale**
  $^1/_2$ **gallon store-bought lime sherbet**
  4 **trays of ice cubes**
    A large sprig of mint

Unwrap sherbet and place mold in the center of the punch bowl. Sprinkle the ice cubes all around it. Slowly pour the two bottles of ginger ale. Garnish with a sprig of mint. The sherbet will slowly melt, and what results is a creamy, delicious soda in a cup. The lime is particularly wonderful because the color is a soft green, but any flavor is great. And it's *so easy!*

SORBETS

Should I, after tea and cakes and ices,
Have the strength to force the moment to its crisis?
—T. S. Eliot, from "The Love Song
of J. Alfred Prufrock," 1917

Sorbets are often called "water ices" or "ices" because they contain no milk. They are characterized by a dense, even intense flavor and a silky smooth texture. They are similar to sherbets, primarily because both are generally made of fruit. Sorbets can be either sweet or savory, and are refreshing between courses during a meal, at a time the French and Italians call an "intermission." (Try our cranberry sorbet next Thanksgiving.) Although sorbets are the ideal low-fat dessert, they are *not* low-calorie.

Sugar water is the sweetening agent for most sorbets. To make sugar water, bring equal parts plain sugar and fresh spring water to a boil and let boil just about a minute, stirring constantly so that the sugar will become completely dissolved. Remove from heat. Cool to room temperature prior to using. The sugar syrup may be refrigerated for several days. If you like a sweeter sorbet, add ½ cup more sugar.

You can certainly use an ice cream maker for sorbets, but it's not necessary. In fact, equipment for sorbets couldn't be simpler: a stainless steel bowl or pan, a wooden or stainless steel spoon, and plastic wrap or matching plastic lid to cover the bowl tightly. Always prepare by pouring boiling water over the stainless steel bowl and the stainless steel or wooden utensils you will use. Wipe dry thoroughly with a clean linen or cotton towel. Do this each and every time; *no exceptions!*

Mixing sorbets (and granitas) is best achieved with a chilled stainless steel fork. The tines in the fork help to reduce crystals and smooth out the mixture better than a spoon or even a hand mixer, which will make the ingredients too thin and unable to solidify enough to the proper texture and consistency.

> *Talking of Pleasure, this moment I was writing with one hand,*
> *and with the other holding to my Mouth a Nectarine—good god,*
> *how fine. It went down soft, pulpy, slushy, oozy—all its*
> *delicious embonpoint melted down my throat like a large*
> *beautified Strawberry.*
>
> —from John Keats, letter to Charles Dilke

BERRY SORBET

Whisk together 1⅓ cups of cooled simple syrup with 1 cup of cold spring water and about 4 pints of puréed fruit (e.g. blackberries or blueberries. Generally, a pound of fruit will equal about 1¼ to 1½ cups of puréed fruit.) Always taste the puréed fruit. Use less syrup if the berries are very sweet; a tablespoon or two more if they are very tart.

Freeze for about 1½ to 2 hours. Using your spoon, scrape the semifrozen mixture from the edge of the bowl, making sure to break up any large pieces. Freeze an additional 2 hours or overnight.

Prior to serving, let sorbet stand at room temperature at least ten minutes. Again, scrape the sorbet from the sides of the bowl, crushing chunks. Process in a bowl and beat for about two minutes. You can put the mixture in a food processor and beat until smooth, but use a stop and start motion to avoid liquefying the mixture. Serve immediately. *Serves about six.*

If you have a freezer machine, follow the directions; the above proportions should work in any machine.

RASPBERRY SORBET

Raspberries are my favorite fruit; I only eat them fresh, and I've been known to pay $5 for a tiny carton. After all, what price pleasure?

At lunch one day at the old Chronicle restaurant in Santa Monica, I was served these edible rubies in a beautiful cut-glass bowl. As I was about to put the first spoonful of delicate berries into my mouth, I caught the eye of a tall, elegant man sitting across the room. He smiled and said, "There's nothing better, is there?" Then he lifted his own heaping spoonful of raspberries, and together we had this mutually orgasmic experience. Sort of a paean to safe sex.

I first learned about dipping strawberries into balsamic vinegar from a real estate client of mine. I couldn't believe something so tart as vinegar could bring out the sweetness of a strawberry so dramatically. I tried it with raspberries, and it works just as well.

4 pints of fresh raspberries (rinse, remove leaves and debris, and air dry)

2 teaspoons balsamic vinegar (only vinegar from Modena is the true balsamic)

2 teaspoons fresh lemon juice

$^1/_2$ cup sugar (or more to taste)

4 wafer cookies

This is so simple, and one of the few recipes that really works well in a blender. Purée the raspberries with the vinegar, lemon juice, and sugar until smooth. Pour mixture through a sieve to eliminate the seeds. Taste; add more sugar if necessary. Freeze in your canister freezer about 4 hours. Present each diner with one large scoop garnished with a crisp wafer cookie. *Serves four.*

BLACK CURRANT SORBET

4 cups black currants, washed clean and dried thoroughly

6 tablespoons water

$^3/_4$ cup sugar (less if currants are very sweet)

1 $^1/_4$ cup water

2 teaspoons fresh lemon juice

Crème de cassis (black currant liqueur)

Gently heat the black currants with 6 tablespoons water in a covered saucepan until fruit is soft and the juices run. Reduce to a purée. Remove from heat and pour through a sieve to remove the seeds.

Dissolve the sugar in 1¼ cups water in a heavy saucepan and bring to a boil for at least ten minutes. Cool slightly and stir in the lemon juice. Strain through a sieve to remove lemon pulp.

Mix the sugar syrup with the black currant purée; hold aside about three tablespoons for garnishing later. Add water to the sugar syrup and purée mixture until you get 3 cups. Pour into a container. Cover and freeze until firm, about 3 hours. Beat three times, once each at 45-minute intervals. Remove the canister from the freezer and place in the refrigerator about 45 minutes prior to serving.

Drizzle crème de cassis over each serving. For a more decadent garnish, mix a tablespoon or two of crème de cassis into whipped cream-making swirls; if you can't resist the pale purple color, whip completely into the whipped cream and garnish each scoop of sorbet with a huge dollop. Then pour a thin line of purée along the edge of the saucer as a decorative and colorful touch. *Serves four.*

Fall Fruit Sorbets

Robert Wemischner is a terrific cooking teacher, an inventive chef, and the author of *Vivid Flavors*, which highlights Pan-Asian cooking. He's also a great enthusiast for fine teas, which is how we met. He graciously contributed the following two sorbet recipes, which show the exquisite way he balances sweet-tart flavors in two of fall's most splendid fruits.

Both recipes include directions for roasting the fruits. Robert says, "The essential fruitiness of the persimmons and pears is enhanced by the roasting process, which concentrates the sugar and flavor components inherent in the fruit and adds some indefinable something to the final product."

PERSIMMON SORBET

1 pound Fuyu persimmons
(the flat variety that can be
eaten while still hard), allowed
to stand at room temperature
until they give easily to light
pressure

¼ cup mild honey (clover, for
example)

Juice of 1 large lemon

2 tablespoons dark rum

Simple syrup to taste (made
from equal parts of granulated
sugar and water, boiled just
until clear, and then cooled
before refrigerating. Keep
refrigerated in a glass jar for
whenever the impulse hits to
turn a seasonable fruit into the
frozen essence of itself.)

Preheat oven to 350° F. You can serve this using the skin of the fruit as a decorative container, which the French call *fruits givres*. Scoop the fruit out of its skin with a spoon, leaving the skin intact as much as possible. Place skin on a cookie sheet and freeze.

Cut peeled fruit into quarters and place on a cookie sheet lightly sprayed with aerosolized vegetable spray. Roast, turning occasionally, for about 15 minutes or until the point of a knife can be easily inserted into the fruit. Although soft, the fruit should retain its shape.

Pour honey evenly over the fruit and continue roasting for about 10 to 15 minutes longer, turning occasionally to be sure that the fruit is not sticking to the pan. Allow to cool. Drizzle with lemon juice and dark rum. Purée in food processor until perfectly smooth, sieving if necessary to remove any remaining solids or fiber. Mix in simple syrup to taste. The mixture should be lightly sweet.

Freeze in an ice cream machine until slushy. Pour into a stainless steel bowl, cover well, and freeze for up to 4 hours or until firm. Fill the frozen persimmon skin shells with the sorbet and serve immediately. *Serves four generously.*

These can be filled ahead of time, frozen, and then allowed to stand at room temperature for about 5 minutes to temper to optimal consistency before serving.

CREAMY CARAMEL PEAR SHERBET

4 large, ripe Bartlett or Comice pears, peeled and cored and quartered to make about 1 1/2 pounds net weight Caramel syrup made from combining 1 cup granulated sugar with 1/2 cup water. Cook syrup without stirring over medium heat in a heavy saucepan, until golden brown

1 cup heavy cream, whipped to soft peaks

GARNISHES
Eau de vie de poire (clear pear brandy). The best comes from Alsace, France, with Oregon producers offering a close second.
Roasted and skinned hazelnuts, coarsely chopped

Preheat oven to 350° F.

Place pears in a heavy sauté pan, lightly sprayed with aerosolized vegetable oil. Roast until tender, about 15 minutes, turning occasionally. Remove from oven, and while still hot, pour caramel over the fruit evenly. Then purée fruit into a food processor. Chill until cold. Freeze in an ice cream machine just until slushy. Fold lightly whipped cream into the pear mixture and then freeze in a stainless steel bowl, tightly covered, for about 4 hours, or until firm. This is best served in the evening on the day it is made but it can hold until the next evening, if necessary. *Serves six generously.*

Citrus Sorbets

Citrus fruits make great sorbets. The following is very refreshing as an "intermission," especially during a meal of roast beef, turkey, or goose.

GRAPEFRUIT ICE

1/2 cup water
3/4 cup granulated sugar (less if
grapefruits are very sweet)
2 cups grapefruit juice,
preferably fresh with pulp

2 tablespoons finely chopped
fresh mint leaves
6 sprigs of mint

Make the sugar syrup. Cool. Combine sugar syrup with grapefruit juice and the chopped mint leaves. Freeze in a freezer-proof container for several hours, or overnight. To serve, place in bowls and garnish with a sprig of mint. This ice looks spectacular in green bowls, from sage to emerald. *Serves six.*

TANGERINE SORBET

Tangerines have that combination of citrus tartness and subtle sweetness that I think is simply divine. Yes, it does takes a little effort to get the juice, but every moment is worth it.

Sugar syrup made with equal
parts of 1/2 cup water and
1/2 cup sugar (see page 86)
2 cups freshly squeezed tangerine
juice, about 8 large tangerines

2 tablespoons finely chopped
tangerine peel (carefully remove
all white pith or sorbet will
be bitter)
6 chocolate wafer cookies

Cool sugar syrup to at least room temperature. Combine with juice and peel. Place in a container and freeze for 4 hours or overnight. Serve with chocolate wafer cookies. *Serves six.*

STORE-BOUGHT

Here is where commercial producers shine. Expert sorbet makers are legion, but here are a few favorites: Savino, based in Michigan; Edy's; Double Rainbow of Northern California; Steve's Homemade Ice Cream, Inc., New York; and most regional brands. As with any other ingredient panel, check the order of ingredients. Fruit should be at least in the top three. If the origin of the fruit is listed, so much the better. Expect both corn syrup and sugar; fruits lose sweetness when frozen with water for ices and sorbets.

Sorbets Like Chefs Make

Here are some sorbet recipes from The Perfect Purée Company's founder, Terry Hayward. If the products aren't sold near you, use frozen fruits, adjusting for sweetness.

CALIFORNIA KIWI SORBET

2¹/₂ cups Perfect Purée
California Kiwi, thawed

³/₄ cup orange juice
1 cup granulated sugar

In a large bowl, combine all ingredients until well blended. Freeze mixture in an ice cream maker according to manufacturer's directions. Serve between courses in the cavity in half of a cantaloupe. For dessert, pair it with sorbets of another fruit, such as cantaloupe or strawberry. *Serves six.*

COCONUT DELUXE SORBET

2 cups Perfect Purée Crazy
Coconut, thawed

1 cup sugar syrup (see page 86)
3 tablespoons lime juice

In a large bowl, combine the purée with the syrup and lime juice, and freeze in an ice cream maker according to manufacturer's directions. *Serves four.*

This looks lovely garnished with blueberries, blackberries, or raspberries and a sprig of mint. Because of the light sweetness of coconut and its pale almost no-color, it blends well with other fruits, like banana, peach, mango, or berry.

(For sources, see references in the back of this book. If the products are not yet available in your area, you can substitute with frozen fruits; always taste and adjust for sweetness.)

GRANITAS

Sister Theresa went to the freezer
To get herself a granita.
When she got there,
The freezer was bare,
'cos Sister Anita had beat 'er.

—Anonymous

Granita is so easy to make, and needs no machinery at all. In fact, all you need is a stainless steel bowl, a freezer, and a fork. A whisk is optional, but it will certainly make the process easier. Granita requires more attention than other confections, as one must beat it every $1/2$ hour to ensure even freezing and the typical granular texture. Never let granita sit; once it has been removed from the freezer to serve, mix once more with a cold fork, scoop out into bowls, and serve immediately.

COFFEE GRANITA

You can add 1¹/₂ tablespoons Kahlua, Tia Maria, or Benedictine in the recipe below, but reduce the sugar to ¹/₄ cup because the liqueur itself is a concentrated sweet taste.

¹/₃ cup sugar	1¹/₄ cups cold water
1¹/₄ fresh, hot, very strong black coffee	4–6 ice cubes
	²/₃ cup heavy cream, whipped

Dissolve sugar into coffee. Add cold water and the ice cubes and stir until the cubes melt. Pour the mixture into a container and cover. Freeze until light crystals form, about 2 hours. Stir the granita and spoon into tall parfait glasses. Top with whipped cream and serve at once. Ice tea spoons are perfect with this. *Serves four.*

CRANBERRY GRANITA

This takes a lot of time for in-and-out of the freezer stirring, but it's so good. It's an ideal "intermission" for meat meals, and certainly fun for cranberry lovers.

1 quart cranberry juice (plain or any combination flavor)	2 tablespoons balsamic vinegar from Modena, Italy; do <u>not</u> substitute
¹/₂ cup sugar syrup (see page 86)	12 vanilla wafer cookies
2 tablespoons freshly-squeezed lemon juice (if lemon is particularly tart, add 1 tablespoon sugar)	1 spring of mint

Chill a 9-by-13-inch metal baking dish, preferably stainless steel. In a medium bowl mix all the ingredients until well blended. Pour into the chilled pan and freeze about thirty minutes, until ice crystals begin to form around the edges of the pan. Remove pan and, with a chilled fork, stir well to incorporate ice back into the mixture. Return to the freezer. Continue to stir about every $\frac{1}{2}$ hour until the mixture becomes thick with the texture of a slush. This will take about 3 hours. Scoop granita out just prior to serving. Clear glass bowls show off the beautiful ruby color. If using as a dessert, garnish with a sprig of mint and a vanilla wafer cookie. *Serves twelve.*

STORE-BOUGHT
Forget about it. Make granitas fresh and serve them promptly.

ICE CREAM DESSERTS

"She was a butterscotch sundae of a woman."
—A. J. Liebling, commenting on
the voluptuous figure of actress
Lillian Russell

Syrups

All the following are suitable for any ice cream dessert or drinks.

Ice cream may be the foundation of great desserts and drinks, but it's a naked confection without the drama of a great syrup.

Hershey's chocolate syrup still tastes great, even if the ingredient panel has more than chocolate these days. Many jam companies make quite serviceable syrups. As always, put your money where your passion for flavor is and buy the best you can afford.

Hot fudge is, well, ambrosia. To make, place fudge topping in a double boiler and heat until warm or place the jar in a pot of very hot water and heat gently.

Butterscotch, strawberry, marshmallow, and a host of commercially made toppings are available and very easy to use. Some manufacturers give directions for heating in the microwave. Follow their directions explicitly.

Don't want to buy commercial products? Homemade jams and fudge syrups are divine.

Chocolate is still the best seller, and it marries well with other flavors like raspberry, coffee, or marshmallow. You could also have pineapple, caramel, hazelnut, or piña colada, or try any of the fine Italian syrups used to flavor soda water. One Kiwi-Rambutan Sundae coming up . . .

Appetite is the best sauce.
—French proverb

BASIC SUNDAE

1 ½ ounces syrup
(your choice of flavor)
2 scoops ice cream
(your choice of flavor)

1 teaspoon crushed peanuts
1 tablespoon whipped cream
1 maraschino cherry

In a chilled oval dish, pour ½ ounce of flavored syrup. Top with two scoops of ice cream. Pour an ounce of syrup on top of the ice cream and sprinkle with crushed peanuts. Add a dollop of whipped cream and a maraschino cherry. Serve with a chilled spoon.

Most sundaes use vanilla ice cream because it's a nice balance to the topping, but choose whatever flavor of ice cream you like. Toppings can match or contrast with the ice cream; it's your call.

BLACK AND WHITE SUNDAE

4 vanilla wafers
1 scoop ice cream
1 scoop chocolate ice cream
Chocolate marshmallow
sauce, to taste

1 teaspoon chopped pecans
1 teaspoon chopped walnuts

Place four vanilla wafers on a flat dish forming two squares. On one of the squares put a scoop of vanilla ice cream with whipped cream on top. Put a scoop of chocolate ice cream on the second square of wafers and pour on chocolate marshmallow sauce. Sprinkle a spoonful of chopped pecans on one side of the dish and chopped walnuts on the other. Serve with a chaser of soda water.

HOBOKEN SUNDAE

A classic dish from Sid's, in Forest Hills (Queens), New York, this is served in the style of a regular sundae only with two scoops of chocolate ice cream topped with rich, thick, pineapple syrup. What made the Hoboken so special was Sid himself. He was a master of sundaes and sodas. He not only created the Hoboken, he jerked the best chocolate egg cream in the universe and used the premier chocolate syrup of all time, Haber's. On a warm Friday night in the 1960s, with the sound of Peter, Paul and Mary singing on the radio, fresh-faced high school kids driving VW Beetles up and down the street saying goodbye friends, and innocence, we prepared for the fall, college, and life ahead.

ICE CREAM MOMENT

Ronald and Phyllis Anatole, Phoenix, Arizona

We love to travel, especially throughout the United States. On one of our driving trips, we stopped in this charming little town called Brookline, near our hometown of Pittsburgh, Pennsylvania. We couldn't resist going into the shops, and one really piqued our interest. It was a combination antique and gift shop, and in the back of the store was a genuine old-fashioned soda fountain.

We were among the first customers that morning and started chatting with the owner, who let us know that she was offering her famous peanut butter sundae on special. It was only 10:00 A.M., but we thought, what the heck? So we sat down on the fountain stools, ordered the sundaes, complete with an incredible peanut butter sauce, and had a delicious time. Which goes to prove that any time is the right time for ice cream.

BASIC BANANA SPLIT

1 ripe banana, firm but not overripe, with no brown spots
3 scoops of ice cream
3 ounces syrup
3 cherries
Whipped cream
2 tablespoons crushed peanuts

Chill an oblong dish. Cut the banana in half. Lay one half on each side of the dish. In the center of the dish place three scoops of ice cream (choose your favorites or make them all vanilla). Pour a different syrup topping onto each of the three scoops, for example, strawberry, chocolate, and butterscotch; add whipped cream and crushed peanuts. Cherries top it off. One for elegance, two for charm, three for symmetry. Serve with a chilled spoon. A tumbler of soda water is a good "chaser."

VARIATION
Some banana split fanatics actually debate whether one should face the cut sides of the banana toward the ice cream (I say yes) or away from the scoops.

In some regions, the banana is used to "hold in" the ice cream. In other areas, a sense of architecture is supplied by adding a pineapple ring in the center of the dish to support the middle scoop, considered critical to the "structure" of the split. A second pineapple ring is cut in half, with one half placed on either side of the middle scoop, to keep the first and third scoops from crashing into one another.

The juice from the pineapple is sprinkled on the banana to keep it from discoloring, although how anyone could resist a split long enough for the banana to turn brown is beyond me.

Some other aficionados find three vanilla scoops unheard-of even if the toppings are varied. They insist on one scoop of vanilla topped by chocolate syrup; one chocolate scoop topped by marshmallow creme, and a scoop of strawberry topped by strawberry preserves or syrup. The nuts, cherries, and whipped cream remain the same.

I find this variation too sweet, but, hey, who am I to argue with tradition?

BASIC PARFAIT

Parfait is a most apt name for this visually pleasing dessert (it means "perfect" in French). Parfaits vary widely, but the following is a typical concoction.

This layered dessert begins with a teaspoon of flavored syrup topped by a scoop of softer, creamier ice cream. Do the layering three times. Top the parfait with an additional teaspoon of syrup, crushed nuts, whipped cream, and a cherry. It's like a vertical banana split without the banana and very pretty. Serve with a soda water chaser. Tall, short-stemmed, fluted parfait glasses are ideal for this but if you do not have them, a tall, narrow tumbler will do.

BROADWAY

Most Broadways are a combination of coffee and chocolate. Some have coffee ice cream with chocolate syrup, others have chocolate ice cream with coffee sprinkles or syrup. The varieties are as vast as the number of soda fountains this country once had.

This particular Broadway is based on recipes of the famed soda fountain chef Louis De Gouy. The man never met a syrup he didn't like and had no concept of "less is more," as evidenced by this dramatic parfait.

1 scoop maple ice cream	Soda spoonful chopped
1 scoop coffee ice cream	walnuts
4 tablespoons whipped cream	Blanched almonds
Soda spoonful chopped	Chocolate syrup
seedless raisins	Butterscotch syrup

Put ice cream into a bowl and add two tablespoons whipped cream, raisins, and walnuts, and mix thoroughly. Coat the inside of a parfait glass with butterscotch syrup and transfer the ice cream mixture to the parfait glass. Top with 2 tablespoons whipped cream and sprinkle with blanched almonds coated in chocolate syrup.

BANANAS FOSTER

This rich dessert was first served in the Commander's Palace restaurant in New Orleans and has become a traditional dessert for this celebratory town. Warning: this is not for the faint-hearted.

¹/₃ cup unsalted butter	¹/₃ cup brandy
¹/₃ cup freshly squeezed orange juice	6 firm bananas, peeled and cut diagonally into two-inch-thick slices
2 tablespoons fresh lemon juice	
³/₄ cup firmly packed brown sugar	1 quart French vanilla ice cream, yours or store-bought
¹/₃ cup banana-flavored liqueur	

In a large skillet, melt butter over medium heat until foam subsides. Stir in orange juice, lemon juice, and sugar and simmer until bubbly, about 3 minutes. You should be able to coat a wooden spoon with the mixture. Do not allow it to burn.

Add liqueur and ignite. When flames subside, add brandy and re-ignite. When flames go out, add the bananas and toss carefully until they are coated.

Spoon sauce and coated bananas over ice cream and serve immediately. *Serves eight.*

PEACHES MELBA

This cosmopolitan dessert was first created in 1891 by the famed French chef Escoffier in honor of Nellie Melba, a magnificent opera singer. She dined at Escoffier's restaurant at the Savoy the day after her acclaimed performance of Elsa in *Lohengrin.* There she was served his creation, which began with carved ice in the shape of a swan covered with spun sugar. In between the wings were fresh peaches and vanilla ice cream. He called it *Les Peches au Cygne* ("peaches of the swan").

Nearly a decade later, for the grand opening of the Carlton Hotel in London in 1899, Escoffier changed the recipe by adding a puree of raspberries to the dish. Melba was one of many celebrities who attended the grand event, and legend has it that she enjoyed the dessert so much she asked what it was called. The chef replied with a question, "May I call it Pêches Melba?" (Peaches Melba) She graciously agreed, and so began a classic one can sing for.

3 cups water	1 cup fresh raspberries, washed, picked over for leaves, and dried
2 cups sugar	
4 large peaches, peeled and halved and pitted	
1 tablespoon natural vanilla extract	1 quart French vanilla ice cream, yours or store-bought

Combine water and sugar and bring to a boil in a medium saucepan. Add peaches and reduce heat to a simmer. Cover the pan and cook for 10 to 15 minutes. Remove from heat and let cool. Stir in vanilla extract and chill mixture.

Heat raspberries to boiling in a small saucepan, mashing them with a wooden spoon and stirring constantly to avoid burning. Remove from the stove and let cool. Chill.

For presentation, place cooked peach halves on chilled dessert plates and top each with a scoop of vanilla ice cream. Drizzle raspberry topping on each. *Serves eight.*

MAKE THAT À LA MODE . . .

Adding a scoop or two of ice cream to a slice of hot apple pie, a peach cobbler, or a thick slab of two-layer chocolate cake could be viewed as, well, overdoing it a bit. But it's really a great balance of the pure simple taste of vanilla ice cream that cuts the richness of pastries. In French, *à la mode* means stylish or fashionable, and we do hope the American fashion of pie à la mode never goes out of style. Yet we have discovered to our chagrin, that the French never eat pie or cake with ice cream. *Très tragique, oui?*

ICE CREAM MOMENT

Kate Grant, Revelation Merchandisers, Sausalito, California

Traveling to France was one of my most memorable vacations. The scenery was breathtaking, the weather was gorgeous, and the food divine. Every great vacation has a "perfect moment" and mine came at lunch one day in Nice. I was seated at an outdoor patio overlooking the sea, and chose—what else?—Salade Niçoise, the eponymous dish of this famous seaside resort. It was an exquisite combination of tuna and anchovies and delicate greens. How could anything be better than that? my companion asked. Wait, I said. We'll try something not yet available in the States, pear sorbet. I had only heard of such perfection, yet my expectation was tentative. I needn't have been concerned. I can still taste it, smooth, not-too-sweet, pure fruity taste, silky down the throat, with just a rumor of nutmeg. A lingering, refreshing aftertaste. Nothing else has even come close.

ICE CREAM DRINKS

I doubt whether the world holds for anyone a more soul-stirring surprise than the first venture into ice cream.
> —Heywood Brown, "Holding the Baby,"
> from *Seeing Things in the Night*

BASIC MILK SHAKE

If you find a diner-style milk shake maker at your next flea market stop, grab it. Nothing makes milk shakes better, although your kitchen blender is a good second choice.

If fat, calories, or cholesterol are no issue to you, you can make a milk shake using 1 cup heavy cream, $\frac{1}{4}$ cup crushed ice, and 1 cup whole milk to 3 tablespoons of flavored syrup and one large scoop of ice cream. The container should be about three-fourths full to accommodate the foam that will occur after mixing. Old-time milk shakes contained buttermilk for extra everything. If you prefer less fat, choose the following recipe.

    1 scoop ice cream
    2 cups whole milk, thoroughly
       chilled (Skim just doesn't do it.)
    3 tablespoons syrup, as desired

Chill the blender jar. Add ice cream and milk. It's important to leave room in the blender jar for the foaming quality of the shake.

    Blend for about 30 seconds until thick and creamy; blending longer will make the mixture too thin. For extra punch, you can add flavored syrup to match the flavor of your ice cream (for instance, a dollop of 3 tablespoons of fudge sauce with chocolate ice cream or a dollop of strawberry jam with strawberry ice cream). Pour into chilled tumbler; top with whipped cream if desired.

BROWN COW MILK SHAKE

2 tablespoons chocolate syrup
1 ½ cups evaporated milk
½ cup Coca-Cola

2 tablespoons crushed ice
Powdered cocoa

Put chocolate syrup into a shaker and add enough evaporated milk to fill half the container; add Coca-Cola until the container is two-thirds full. Add crushed ice and shake vigorously or mix in a milk shake machine. Pour into a glass through a strainer. Dust the top with powdered cocoa.

Note: Some allege that a brown cow is *only* a soda made with vanilla ice cream and Coca-Cola. So much depends upon where you live in the United States. In the South, Coca-Cola is the predominant soda used; in the North and Midwest, it is root beer. Please, don't write.

COCOA CHOCO SHAKE

This drink is built like a parfait; however, the chilling mélange of flavors is best savored as a thoroughly mixed cold drink.

1 tablespoon chocolate syrup
1 scoop mocha ice cream
½ teaspoon very finely ground espresso
1 scoop French vanilla ice cream, with vanilla bean bits
1 scoop premium-grade chocolate ice cream

GARNISHES
Roughly broken dark chocolate candy bar, about two ounces
Real whipped cream, about 2 tablespoons

Build the parfait in the order in which the ingredients are listed above except for the garnishes. To serve, garnish with a dollop of real whipped cream and the chocolate. To serve as a shake, put all of the ingredients, except the whipped cream and candy bar, into the shaker or blender jar, beat for thirty seconds, and pour into a frosty-cold glass. Top with the whipped cream and chocolate bits.

For wintertime, the completely mixed ingredients, including the chocolate bits, may be heated gently in a heavy saucepan for about five minutes; do not boil. Serve in preheated ceramic mugs, topped with whipped cream. Additional chocolate pieces can be sprinkled over the whipped cream.

Java Latté Shake

4 cups coffee ice cream	Whipped cream
3 tablespoons brewed espresso or strong coffee	Ground cinnamon, cardamom or nutmeg to taste

Whirl together the ice cream and coffee in a blender until just mixed. Pour into chilled tumblers and top with whipped cream and dust with your choice of flavoring: cinnamon, cardamom, or nutmeg.

Basic Malt

Malts are made just like milk shakes, except that malted milk powder is added. It's available at any supermarket. Use about three teaspoons or to taste. My favorite is chocolate; so what else is new?

1 scoop chocolate ice cream	3 teaspoons of malted milk powder
1½ cups very cold milk	
1 tablespoon chocolate syrup	Whipped cream

Put the first four ingredients in the jar, making sure there's at least one-fourth to one-third space left in jar to accommodate foam. Whip in blender or milk shake machine, pour into a chilled glass, and top with whipped cream.

SILVER SLAMMER

Cathy Brown, whose sinful peach ice cream is included in this book, has agreed to share her heretofore secret recipe for Silver Slammers. She suggests that anyone drinking this not operate heavy equipment for twenty-four hours. *Take her word for it.*

1 pint French vanilla ice cream (the richer the better)
$^1/_2$ cup brandy
$^1/_4$ cup coffee liqueur
$^1/_2$ cup genuine chocolate morsels

Place all ingredients in a blender and mix until all blended and creamy. Serve in chilled parfait glasses with a straw and long spoon. Garnish with shaved chocolate or additional chocolate morsels. *Serves four.*

BASIC ICE CREAM SODA

To preserve your health during the warm season, drink from two to five glasses of Dow's Ice Cream Soda Water daily.
—Advertisement for G. D. Dow's Drugstore, 1861

Philadelphia, home to so many ice cream creations, is also the birthplace of the man who created the ice cream soda, Robert M. Green. During the October 1874 semicentennial celebration of the Franklin Institute in his hometown, Green was selling cream sodas, made with cream and soda water. Due to the popularity of the event, he quickly ran out of cream. In a flash of genius, he substituted vanilla ice cream for the cream, and another American tradition was born.

1 1/2 ounces flavored syrup
2 1/2 scoops ice cream
    Whipped cream

Soda water or carbonated
water, chilled

Using a chilled tumbler or soda glass, pour syrup into the bottom of the glass; add a very small scoop of ice cream and a tablespoon of whipped cream. Pour in chilled soda or carbonated water until the glass is about three-fourths full. Add a full scoop of ice cream and top it off with more whipped cream. Place the second full scoop of ice cream on the rim of the glass and tamp down. If this is too precious for you, add the two full scoops of ice cream in the glass prior to adding the whipped cream. A long iced tea or soda spoon is a must and a paper straw essential.

BLACK COW

1 1/2 ounces root beer syrup
  1 tablespoon whipped cream
    Carbonated water

2 scoops vanilla ice cream
  Whipped cream for topping

In a cold soda glass, put in the root beer syrup and add the whipped cream. Fill the glass to about three-fourths full with carbonated water. Gently place the scoops of vanilla ice cream. Add more soda water if necessary to top the glass and splurge with a topping of whipped cream.

BROADWAY: SODA VERSION

The Broadway appears as a name for parfaits, sundaes, and sodas but the following is the suggested recipe for the soda version.

1 1/2 ounces chocolate syrup
1 teaspoon coffee cream, or whipped cream

2 scoops coffee ice cream
Carbonated water
Whipped cream

In a cold soda glass, put in the chocolate syrup and add the coffee cream or whipped cream. Fill the glass to about three-fourths full with carbonated water. Gently place the scoops of coffee ice cream. Add more soda water if necessary to top the glass and splurge with a topping of whipped cream.

HOT ICE CREAM SODA

This anomaly was invented in 1964 in response to a request by actor Burgess Meredith; this H. Hicks of Manhattan soda gained tremendous popularity after appearing in the New York *Herald-Tribune.* For those who think latté is so new, try this thirty-four-year-old recipe!

1/2 cup cocoa
1 cup fresh hot coffee
1 tablespoon heavy cream, whipped

1 scoop coffee ice cream
(or your choice of flavor)

Put hot coffee over the cocoa and blend well. Put ice cream in a soda glass with a metal spoon. Pour hot mixture into the jar (the spoon will prevent any breakage of glass). Like magic, the ice cream will float to the top. Zap it with whipped cream and serve immediately.

BASIC FRAPPÉ

This is basically a slush made with sherbet.

3 scoops of sherbet

Mix three scoops of sherbet in a blender for only about twenty seconds; pour into a chilled tumbler or soda glass, and drink slowly.

THE MANZI

Carolyn Manzi is a bead jewelry designer with a decidedly whimsical and colorful style that she translates to her cooking, making her a sought-after personal chef. The following is her favorite rendition of a frappé.

**2 scoops fruit sorbet
(anything from mango
to berry to orange, whatever
pleases you)**

**1 1/2 cups sparkling water, chilled
(lemon-, orange- or
lime-flavored are good
choices)**

In a blender jar, put in two scoops of fruit sorbet. Add chilled sparkling water and whip in a blender. Pour into a large tumbler or a large globe glass.

The flavored mineral water cuts the sweetness of the sorbet and produces a tart-sweet drink that's very refreshing. Can also be served like a soda without blending. It's as pretty to look at as it is delicious to eat.

SAVINO RASPBERRY CORDIAL SMOOTHIE

The following is the creation of Lou DeCillis, who dishes out nearly a half-million pints of his Savino Frozen Desserts every year, including fat-free ice cream and fruit sorbets that please even Hillary and Bill. His sorbets and fat-free ice creams are available in Michigan and at most Kroger, Shopping Center markets, and Arbor Drugs. (For more information, call (800) CHEF-LOU.)

I've already professed my love affair with raspberries. This is coupled with my second love, chocolate. To live for!

8 ounces Savino Raspberry Sorbet	3 ounces skim milk
	3 ounces sparkling water
2 ounces chocolate syrup	1 medium banana, cut up

Whirl all ingredients in a blender only until just blended. This tastes best when still "lumpy" and thick like a shake.

HÄAGEN-DAZS CHOCOLATE SORBET SODA FLOAT

This chocolate sorbet is perfect. Fortunately, it's available everywhere frozen desserts are sold, and in two forms, on a stick and in pints. It has just the right intensity of chocolate flavor to truly satisfy. Here, we make a great thing greater.

8 ounces Häagen-Dazs Chocolate Sorbet	6 ounces soda water
	2 ounces raspberry syrup

Whirl all ingredients in a blender just until mixed. For creamier soda, substitute 3 ounces of soda water with 3 ounces of low-fat or whole milk. Other flavors of syrup that go well with chocolate are coffee and, you guessed it, chocolate.

DOUBLE RAINBOW MARION BLACKBERRY SHAKE

This always immediately takes me to Ashland, Oregon, to the Shakespeare festival and the fine restaurants in that charming town. Oregon has the *best* berries, but the marion berry is the ultimate.

8 ounces Double Rainbow Marion Blackberry Sorbet

2 ounces orange juice
4 ounces skim milk

Whirl all ingredients in blender only until just mixed. You can substitute some Calistoga Berry Sparkling water for the skim milk.

BASIC FLOAT

I maintain that a float is a variation on a soda, although some people swear it's a category of its own. Floats are made by "floating" a small dip of ice cream onto soda water previously mixed in an ordinary ice cream soda. (Just think of it like a "starter" for bread. It adds extra sweetness and flavor versus the tang of plain soda.) It's also sweeter than a regular soda, and that's why root beer is often used instead of soda water.

2 scoops ice cream or sherbet
1 1/2 cups soda water

Put a large tablespoon of ice cream and two tablespoons of the "starter" soda into a chilled tumbler or large glass mug. Add the rest of the ice cream or sherbet with enough fresh soda water to enable the scoops to float to the top.

To gild the lily, put on some whipped cream. Ya gotta have a straw and a long-handled spoon. It's the rule.

BLACK COW

1 $\frac{1}{2}$ cups root beer (A&W, what else?)
  2 scoops vanilla ice cream
    Whipped cream

Fill a glass three-fourths full with root beer and add ice cream. Top with whipped cream. Serve with long-handled spoon and straw. If you've never had an A&W Root Beer Float, you don't know what a float is!

BROADWAY

The Broadway can be made as an ice cream soda, a malt, a shake, or a float, but basically it has the same primary ingredients: coffee ice cream and chocolate syrup, an ambrosial combination of flavors.

    Soda water
  2 scoops chocolate ice cream
  1 tablespoon chocolate syrup
    Whipped cream

For a Broadway soda, fill a chilled glass three-fourths full with soda water and add chocolate ice cream and chocolate syrup. Top with whipped cream, if desired. Serve with long-handled spoon and straw.

BROWN COW

1 ½ cups Coca-Cola (nothing else will do—stalwarts aver)
2 scoops vanilla ice cream
Whipped cream

Fill a glass three-fourths full with Coca-Cola and add ice cream. Top with whipped cream. Serve with long-handled spoon and straw. If you live in the South, soda *is* Coca-Cola.

CAPPUCCINO FLOAT

This is so-o-o-o great in warm weather or cool, especially if you love cappuccino.

1 scoop vanilla ice cream
(if you're a coffee addict,
use coffee ice cream)
1 measuring cup of cappuccino
(8 ounces)

Soda water
Whipped cream
Powdered nutmeg, cocoa,
or espresso

Into a heat-proof glass, add a large scoop of premium vanilla or coffee ice cream, pour in your prepared cup of cappuccino, and add soda water to fill the glass. Stir one time, slowly. Top with whipped cream, as desired. Sprinkle with nutmeg, cocoa, or finely-ground espresso.

GINGER BEER FLOAT

Ginger beer is a ginger ale with considerably more bite from the ginger in it. We first tried the following combination at San Francisco's Shanghai 1930 restaurant, which served it in mini soda glasses. Way too small . . .

    2 scoops Ciao Bella Tahitian Vanilla Gelato
    12 ounces ginger beer, icy cold

Put a tablespoon of the ice cream in glass. Pour in a tablespoon of ginger beer and stir. Add the rest of the ice cream, and fill the glass to the top with the ginger beer. A little whipped cream is always nice, but not necessary.

The creamy sweet richness of the best-grade vanilla gelato balances the tart bite of the ginger beer.

If you're too wussy for ginger beer, ginger ale is great, but use a vanilla ice cream that is less rich than the gelato. Otherwise, the float is simply too sweet. If you can't find vanilla gelato, premium French vanilla ice cream is just fine.

If you just have to have your own vanilla gelato, try this one; make sure to use a wooden spoon and either Pyrex bowls or stainless steel bowls:

VANILLA GELATO

5 large egg yolks
³/₄ cup sugar
2 cups whole milk

1 cup half-and-half
2 teaspoons pure vanilla extract

In a medium bowl beat together the egg yolks with the sugar until thick and creamy yellow in color. In a saucepan, warm the milk to barely a simmer and add one cup of it to the egg yolk and sugar mixture. Whisk until blended, then slowly stir in the remaining cup of milk. Cook this blended mixture over low heat, stirring constantly until the mixture coats the back of your wooden spoon. Remove from heat and gently stir in the half-and-half. Set a bowl over an ice bath* to chill, and sieve the mixture into the bowl. Stir in the vanilla, pour the cooled mixture into your ice cream freezer canister, and freeze according to manufacturer's instructions. Makes about one quart which serves about ten.

   *An ice bath is a bowl or deep pan filled with ice and ice water used to cool down a heated mixture prior to freezing it, thus avoiding curdling, lumps, or other aggravations of temperature changes.

FROZEN YOGURT

This is a rather odd frozen dessert category. Using true yogurt culture makes a tangy, even sour tasting product; adding lots of sugar adds tons of calories and completely changes the very nature of a yogurt culture, but, hey, it's fun to experiment.

This tastes best with fresh homemade yogurt, but good-quality commercial brands abound. Look for those that do not have stabilizers in the ingredients. Homemade yogurts will not have the consistency of commercial frozen yogurt, but will be softer, tangier, and more healthful. Adding more sugar than suggested is always an option, but do not use honey as the consistency will change.

For all the frozen yogurt recipes, make a yogurt cheese first. Put the yogurt into a fine-mesh sieve or cheesecloth, and let drain over a bowl for about 20 minutes. Gently squeeze the "cheese" to remove any remaining liquid. This results in a creamier, thicker base for your frozen yogurt.

BASIC FROZEN YOGURT

6 cups fresh plain yogurt cheese (continental or Bulgarian style)
1 1/2 teaspoons natural vanilla extract

Mix the yogurt and vanilla and freeze in a hand-cranked or electric ice cream freezer according to manufacturer's directions. (If you want a sweeter taste, add 1/2 cup of sugar.)

BERRY FROZEN YOGURT

5 cups fresh plain yogurt cheese (continental or Bulgarian style)
1 cup sugar
1 cup puréed frozen berries

Mix the yogurt, sugar, and puréed berries thoroughly and freeze in a hand-cranked or electric ice cream freezer according to manufacturer's directions. (If you want to use fresh fruit, wash and dry it thoroughly, then let it rest at room temperature in 2 tablespoons of the sugar to bring out its natural sweetness. Continue with the recipe as shown.)

COFFEE FROZEN YOGURT

5 cups plain fresh yogurt cheese (continental or Bulgarian style)
1 cup sugar
$^1/_2$ cup instant espresso or dark roast coffee (brewed coffee tends to make the yogurt too thin. If the flavor is too intense, use $^1/_4$ cup of instant coffee with $^1/_4$ cup real chocolate morsels and cut back the sugar to $^3/_4$ cup)

Mix the yogurt, sugar, and coffee thoroughly and freeze in a hand-cranked or electric ice cream freezer according to manufacturer's directions.

ICE CREAM MOMENT

Marie Henry, who lives in California and ate 50–50s growing up,
now swears by Breyer's Mint Chocolate Chip

You can always tell whether someone grew up in the East or in the West. Just ask them what you call a combination of orange sherbet and vanilla ice cream on a stick. If they say a Creamsicle, they're from "back east." If they say a 50–50, they're from out west. It works every time.

DIETETIC DELIGHTS

Do you really want to know the calories in frozen desserts? It seems a bit self-defeating, but here's the scoop. Note the serving size. A pint of frozen dessert has eight ounces. Calories will be higher with sweeter ingredients, including fruit.

Ice cream has 140 calories, 15 grams of carbohydrates, 7 grams of fat, and 30 milligrams of cholesterol per ½ cup or 2.2-ounce serving. The percentage of calories from fat is 45 percent.

Sherbet has 135 calories, 29 grams of carbohydrates, 2 grams of fat, and 7 milligrams of cholesterol. The percentage of calories from fat is 8 percent per ½ cup serving of 3 ounces. You get almost the same amount of calories here, but not as much fat; you choose.

Frozen yogurt has 90 calories, 19 grams of carbohydrates, 3.5 grams of fat, and 7 milligrams of cholesterol with 7 percent of calories from fat. The serving size is ½ cup or 3.5 ounces.

Sorbet has 90 calories, 17 grams of carbohydrates, and 0 grams of fat or cholesterol for a 3-ounce serving made with sugar and fruit. Some sorbets have more calories when sweeter fruit is used.

I am a gourmet
YOU are a gourmand
HE is fat
—Craig Brown, the *New York Times,*
November 1989

LACTOSE-FREE, LOW-FAT, AND LOW-SUGAR FROZEN DESSERTS

The ounce sizes vary even though the cup size remains the same because of the weight of the fat.

Lactose-Free

More than 70 percent of the world's population does not drink milk or eat milk products except an occasional aged cheese. Scandinavians and north Europeans like the British are the only groups that have milk as a regular part of their diet.

Most other ethnic groups have been found to be lactose-intolerant. This medical condition is the inability to digest milk sugar (lactose), milk protein (lactalbumin), or both, in milk or milk products because the proper enzyme levels are not present. Nearly everyone in the world loses enzyme levels as they age, so elderly people can sometimes become lactose-intolerant even if they were not when they were young.

What if you crave a frozen dessert but are lactose intolerant? For most people with this condition, granitas, slushes, and sorbets are the simplest and easiest frozen desserts to use, preferably homemade. Commercial and restaurant-made sorbets *may* contain some milk solids in them as binders, so ask before ordering; granitas and slushes seem to pose no problem.

If it's a creamy dessert that you want, consider rice milk. It is an ideal milk substitute, universally accepted by all because it has no milk protein. Best of all, it offers the smooth, creamy texture that people enjoy from an ice cream, but without the lactose.

Legumes, like soybeans (from which tofu is made) and soy milk, contain protein. Anyone allergic to peanuts, which is not a nut but a legume, may also be allergic to soy products, another reason to choose only rice milk products as an ice cream substitute or to stick with frozen desserts like sorbets and granitas.

Some commercial lactose-free ice cream products found in most health food stores or supermarkets are Ice Bean, Rice Dream, Tofutti, Dole Fruit Sorbets, and Mocha Mix. Many others are available; *always* read the label of any new product you try.

On all frozen dessert products, lactose-intolerant shoppers should look for these words or phrases: *reduced lactose milk* or *milk solids, casein, milk solids, milk proteins, milk sugars, lactose.* If any of them is listed on the label of ingredients, do not buy the product.

> *"There," said the Lord Abbot, "we shall not starve; God's bounties are great, it is fit we should enjoy them."*
> —William Beckford, "Recollections of an excursion to the monasteries of Alcobaca and Batalha," 1794

Fat-Free

For fat-free desserts, sorbets or granitas and most sherbets fit the bill without any substitutions. Be aware that most commercial products contain considerably more sugar than homemade frozen desserts. Low-fat milk can be used with many of our ice creams, but skim and 1 percent do not work well.

> *Ice cream is a delicious, nutritious dessert. It was never intended to be a main course.*
> —Thomas Palchak, University Creamery, Penn State University

Sugar-Free

Those who are watching their sugar intake because of calories have many options. A milk shake with unsweetened fruit and ice cubes blended in makes a refreshing, nonfat drink. Adding a cut-up date or prune or pear juice can add the right amount of sweetening to ice creams and frozen yogurts, and many fruit sorbets or frozen fruit bars have reduced sugar, fructose, or pear juice as a sweetener.

These substitutions, however, should *not* be used by diabetics, for they must be careful to weigh all sweeteners against their overall menu plans for the day.

Some commercial sugar-free products to check out with your doctor are Baskin-Robbins and Dreyer's Grand sugar-free ice cream and Mrs. Tisch's Italian Ices. (Most are okay for diabetics but it's always a good idea to get your nutritionist or doctor's input.)

Although some diabetics can digest fruits or fructose readily, others can use only synthetic sweeteners like Aspartame or saccharin, and in small quantities. Sugar alcohols like sorbitol, malitol, and xylitol are sometimes used in sugar-free products. They are considered sugarless sweeteners, which are extracts of ethyl alcohol but do not get absorbed or digested like regular sugars. To substitute for sugar in our regular recipes, use half the sugar quantity suggested for fructose or the sugar equivalent of artificial sweeteners (check the packages of your favorite brands to get reliable equivalencies).

When using custard-based ice creams, add artificial sweeteners *after* the custard has cooled, or the ice cream will have a bitter taste. Note: Fats will diminish the flavor of artificial sweeteners but fruits will enhance their flavor. Adjust accordingly.

Seaweed sugars and stevia are natural and have no side effects, making them easy to digest. In time, they will become more available; until then, commercial synthetic sweeteners are the only answer for the diabetic who has a craving for something sweet other than fresh fruit.

Sugars come with many names so it's critical to read labels of commercial products if you are diabetic. Some terms to look for are: *sugar, turbinado sugar, beet sugar, corn syrup, corn sugar, raw sugar, fructose, lactose, sucrose.*

RECIPES FOR SPECIAL NEEDS

(**ND**: not for use by a diabetic; **D**: acceptable for most diabetics) **If you are a diabetic, please consult your nutritionist or physician before trying any of the desserts listed here with a D.** All others, in this section and throughout this book, should **not** be used by a diabetic.

RHUBARB CREAM (D)

1 pound rhubarb, trimmed and cut into chunks (if frozen, defrost and drain thoroughly)	½ cup low-fat plain yogurt
	½ cup low-fat cottage cheese
1 cup raspberries, picked over and cleaned	12 drops liquid sweeteneer, or to taste
	2 egg whites

If using fresh rhubarb, put into water and bring to a boil. Cook until tender, about 8 minutes. Cool and drain. Blend into a purée with a food processor or a blender with ½ cup fresh raspberries.

Put rhubarb mixture into a glass bowl and beat in the plain yogurt and the cottage cheese. Stir in sweetener to taste. (If sugar is not a problem, add four teaspoons of sugar instead of the artificial sweetener.)

In another bowl, preferably copper or glass, beat the egg whites with a pinch of salt until stiff peaks form. Gently fold the egg whites into the rhubarb and raspberry mixture. No need to freeze. Simply pour into parfait glasses or glass serving bowls, garnish with the remaining raspberries, and serve. Can be chilled up to 2 hours before serving. Garnish at the last moment, if not serving promptly. *Serves four.*

DONVIER'S SUGAR-FREE ICE CREAM (D)

1 egg	6 packages Equal
1 1/2 cups milk	1 teaspoon vanilla extract

If you're not counting calories, you can combine 3/4 cup each of milk and cream for a richer dessert. You can also use 3/4 cup fruit and 3/4 cup milk for a flavored ice cream. Beat all the ingredients together and pour into your Donvier or other canister unit.

PUMPKIN ICE CREAM (D)

1 egg	1/2 cup milk
5 packages Equal	1/2 cup solid packed fresh
1/2 teaspoon cinnamon	pumpkin*
1/8 teaspoon ginger	3/4 cup cream
Dash of ground cloves	

Beat the egg and add the Equal. Add all the rest of the ingredients except the cream and blend well. Gently fold in the cream, and place in your canister unit and freeze according to manufacturer's directions.

*Be cautious about canned pumpkin; many are already seasoned with the above spices, and some contain additional sugars, so fresh is best.

FROZEN FRUIT YOGURT (D)

1 1/2 cups yogurt
1/2 cup fruit juice (If your diet limits fruit juice, replace with 1/2 cup yogurt.)
5 packages Equal

This is a really smooth, creamy frozen yogurt, softer than usual but quite yummy. Simply add yogurt and fruit juice together and stir in sweetener. Freeze as you would in any canister system. If sugar is not an issue, $^1/_3$ cup sugar can be substituted for the artificial sweetener.

CANTALOUPE AND PEACH YOGURT (ND)

2 ripe peaches
1 medium cantaloupe
2 tablespoons blanched sliced
  almonds

1 cup white sugar
$^2/_3$ cup plain low-fat yogurt
2 egg whites

Peel, skin, and pit peaches. Cut cantaloupe and remove seeds; cut melon meat from skin. Put melon and peaches with almonds into a food processor or blender and blend until smooth, but not too thin; it should have the consistency of a purée. Stir in sugar and yogurt until well blended. Pour into a bowl, cover, and freeze until the consistency of a slush, about 1 hour.

In a glass or copper bowl, beat egg whites until frothy, then fold them into the partially frozen fruit mixture. Return to the freezer and freeze until firm, about 2 more hours, or put into a canister freezer and follow the directions.

Just prior to serving, remove the yogurt and let it soften just slightly. Spoon into tall glasses or parfait glasses, and decorate with fresh mint. *Serves four.*

CHOCOLATE TOFU ICE CREAM (ND)

20 ounces drained silky tofu
 2 teaspoons pure vanilla extract
$^2/_3$ cup sugar syrup (see page 86)
 6 ounces semi-sweet chocolate, melted

To drain tofu, place a strainer inside a large bowl. Place the tofu in the strainer and cover tofu with a heavy plate to help press out liquid. Set aside for about 15 minutes, to allow excess water to run off. Discard liquid and use the tofu, which will be slightly more solid. The creamier, silky tofu makes a nicer texture than firm-brick tofu, but either can be used.

Purée tofu in blender and add vanilla and sugar syrup. Add melted chocolate. Scrape blender jar and mix thoroughly. Pour mixture into ice cream freezer container and follow manufacturer's directions. *Serves six.* This does not keep well, so use the same day as you make it.

STRAWBERRY TOFU ICE CREAM (ND)

1 ¼ cups puréed strawberries
1 ¼ cups tofu
1 tablespoon fructose, about
Few drops of pure vanilla
extract

Four strawberries, halved,
stems removed

Pour strawberry purée through strainer to remove seeds. Put purée into a blender with tofu, fructose, and vanilla and blend until smooth. Pour into a container, cover, and freeze until firm. Beat twice at 60-minute intervals. About 30 minutes prior to serving, transfer from the freezer to the refrigerator. Scoop into small bowls and garnish with fresh strawberries. *Serves four.*

SOYBEAN MILK AND TOFU ICE CREAM WITH CAROB (ND)

3 tablespoons unsweetened
carob powder
1 pound soft tofu
1 cup unflavored soybean milk
½ cup vegetable oil

⅓ cup brown sugar
Few drops of pure vanilla
or almond extract
Four sprigs of mint

Mix all the ingredients (except mint) together in a blender until smooth. Pour into a container, cover, and freeze until firm, beating the mixture three times at intervals of 45 minutes each. About 30 minutes before serving, transfer container to the refrigerator. Scoop out into bowls and garnish with mint sprigs. *Serves four.*

Glossary

. . . .

à la mode An addition of a scoop or two of ice cream to a baked dessert, usually pie or cake.

acque or aqua gelate water ice (*see* **eaux glacées**)

black and white A sundae made with vanilla ice cream with whipped cream and chocolate ice cream with marshmallow sauce. Chopped nuts are sprinkled on top and the entire dish is served atop vanilla wafers. Previously, it was a soda made with chocolate malted milk or chocolate soda with vanilla ice cream.

Black Cow A soda made with a combination of root beer and vanilla ice cream. Depending on the region in which you live, it can also be made with root beer, evaporated milk, chocolate syrup, powdered cocoa, and crushed ice.

bombe These were enormously popular in the era of excess known as the Victorian age. Elaborately shaped molds were so varied that London shopkeeper Agnes Marshall carried hundreds. The shaped and layered molded iced dessert is usually composed of two or more flavors or textures. The jacket, the outer case, is a harder ice and the inner layer, the softer ice. The word "bombe" is the dessert and the name of the domelike mold used to create it. Bombe molds are usually made of copper with a tight-fitting lid and sometimes a screw-on pedestal or little feet to enable the bombe mold to stand upright while freezing. Many shapes were named for women of that era; how the shape of the bombe related to the women, we are uncertain. A number of the recipes remain, e.g., Coppelia (coffee jacket with praline center), Marie-Louise (chocolate with vanilla center), and Josephine (pistachio with coffee jacket).

Broadway Any of an assortment of frappés, sodas, sundaes, or banana splits made with a combination of chocolate and coffee ice creams and syrups.

brown and white A sundae made with a combination of vanilla and chocolate ice cream and marshmallow and chocolate syrup.

Brown Cow A soda made with Coca-Cola and vanilla ice cream. Many variations abound, some adding chocolate syrup or cocoa, depending on the region.

butterfat This is the part that makes ice cream creamy. Most states require a product to be at least 10 percent butterfat to be called ice cream; most quality manufacturers use from 12 to 14 percent, and premium products can have as high as 16 to 22 percent butterfat. It serves more than the taste satisfaction quotient; it also helps to balance the ingredients in the mix. Also known as *milk fat*.

carrageenan An extract of a marine plant called Irish Moss, carrageenan is a natural stabilizer used to prevent separation during the liquid process of ice cream making. It also gives frozen desserts a creamier texture. Irish Moss grows off the coast of New England in the United States and along the coasts throughout Europe.

coupe The container of either glass or silver-plated metal used to serve a sundae or other ice cream dessert. It is often cuplike in shape and has a footed or pedestal stand.

cream ice A sorbet mixed with whipped cream.

Creamsicle Generally, this is a frozen treat on a stick, with orange sherbet covering vanilla ice cream; also made in strawberry over vanilla. In the western United States this dessert was known as the 50-50; many copies of the concept have been made from Häagen-Dazs and lesser-known companies.

Creme à la Moscovite A popular Victorian dessert that was more a jelly than an ice cream because it included gelatin, was molded and was served soft-frozen after being cooled in an ice cave only a few hours. Rarely made today, it is included here only to intrigue you.

dasher The paddle in an ice cream freezer, usually wood, but sometimes plastic. Must be flexible enough to scrape the ice cream from the side of the container and keep it mixed.

eaux glacées or eaux d'Italie   The name of water ices when they first gained popularity in the early 1660s in France, Italy, and Spain.

emulsifier   This element helps keep the butterfat spread evenly throughout the ice cream instead of congealing in spots. Natural emulsifiers are lecithin and egg yolks; other emulsifiers are known as mono- and diglycerides and are also natural derivatives of the fat from vegetable oils and soybeans.

Eskimo Pie   The creation of candy maker Russell Stover and ice cream maker Christian Nelson, this was the original chocolate-covered ice cream bar; first invented in 1921. By 1922 the bar's manufacturer sold more than 1 million "pies" per day. The patent was proved invalid and there were many versions, namely, **the Good Humor Bar**. An "Eskimo Pie" is still marketed today, but there are many copies of the type of ice cream treat.

fat free   Throughout this book, I recommend sorbets and granitas over fat-free anything because of the typical presence of chemicals. But if you can't resist, know that the United States Food and Drug Administration (FDA) guidelines require less than .5 grams of fat per serving for a product to be classified as fat free. Look for the FDA rating to be sure.

float   An ice cream soda with flavoring, soda water, and ice cream, whipped and poured into a glass which is edged with another scoop of ice cream. There are as many variations of this drink as Howard Johnson had flavors; see our version on page 109.

frappé   Purée of fruit frozen with water and blended to be a drink; great way to enjoy a granita or sorbet that hasn't hardened sufficiently.

French vanilla   This is a rich vanilla that is made with more cream, egg yolks for added texture, creamy pale yellow color, and extra flavor. Generally, United States manufacturers must use a minimum of 1.4 percent egg yolk solids to qualify an ice cream as French vanilla. Upscale products usually contain real vanilla bean, but it is not a requirement. Flecks of brown are typical of **Philadelphia ice creams** that use real vanilla bean.

Fudgsicle   A chocolate sherbet on a stick. This confection is now owned and distributed by the Nestlé Company.

gelati/gelato   An Italian custard-based ice cream dessert made with considerably less air to provide a densely flavored, rich taste because it contains more eggs but, ironically, less cream. Available commercially and in Italian grocery stores.

Good Humor Bar   One of the many knockoffs of the original chocolate-covered vanilla ice cream bar on a stick, **Eskimo Pie**, Good Humor was developed by Harry Burt Sr., a candy man, one of many to get involved in ice cream. It still sells well today; currently produced and distributed by Breyer's Ice Cream.

granita   An edible slush, usually made with sugar syrup and flavoring that is served in a bowl or parfait glass. It is an excellent alternative to milk-based frozen desserts because it can be made without a traditional ice cream machine or freezer, and made in less time. Because it takes less sugar than sorbet, it is also lower in calories. Too much sugar would make it lose its classic granular texture. It should be eaten the day it is made. It is the frozen dessert most like the first ever made by man.

guar gum   A product of the seed of the guar plant, guar gum is a natural complex carbohydrate that adheres water molecules to an ice cream mixture during the freezing process. The gum, a native of India, is used in a powdered form and helps to create a smooth texture.

Hoboken   A pineapple ice cream soda made with chocolate milk. My agent likes this one.

hokey pokey   A cheap version of the **Neapolitan** "brick" of three different ice cream flavors. The legend goes that Italian ice cream vendors used to bark their wares with the phrase, *Ecco un poco* (eat a little thing) or *Che un poco*. It's reasonable to assume that the English-speaking Americans could change that to Hokey Pokey. The vendors would slice off a small piece from the ice cream brick, wrap it up in paper, and sell it for pennies.

hot fudge sundae   A sundae made with vanilla ice cream and chocolate fudge sauce that has been warmed prior to pouring over the ice cream. Chopped peanuts, whipped cream, and the maraschino cherry are de rigeur.

ice cave   A precursor of the ice cream freezer, not unlike an ice box, used to freeze ice cream and sorbets during the late 1800s.

ice cream   A dessert made with milk, sugar, and flavoring and frozen to a solid state. It is sometimes made with a custard base using eggs.

ice cream soda   An ice cream drink made with two scoops of ice cream and topped with plain soda. It is sometimes gilded with the addition of whipped cream. It can be eaten with a long-handled spoon or sipped through a straw.

ice cream sundae   An ice cream dessert made with ice cream and a sweet topping. It is frequently served with a garnishing of chopped peanuts and the ubiquitous maraschino cherry.

jerk   Not a criticism of character, but the person behind the soda fountain who "jerks" the handles to pour out soda into floats and sodas, and who whips up other ice cream confections.

kulfi   An ice cream dessert from India that is a rich, thick custardlike confection usually made with pistachio, almond, cashew, raisin, mango, and saputo (a Chinese fruit that also grows in India). Commercially made kulfi is available at most Indian grocery stores.

lactose   Milk sugar that occurs naturally in milk and all milk-based foods. It is a simple carbohydrate and is difficult for some people to digest. It should be considered a sugar by those who must watch their sugar intake. Other sugars are *fructose, sucrose, corn syrup,* and *corn sugar.*

malt   An ice cream drink, similar to a milk shake, but with the addition of powdered malt, usually chocolate or vanilla flavor.

milkshake   An ice cream drink made with milk and ice cream and blended in a shaker, either electric or hand operated. It should be thick, creamy, and icy cold.

Neapolitan   Although originally made in the mid-nineteenth century with wild colors and different flavors, this Italian ice cream is now sold as a large rectangular brick with three flavors layered one atop the other: chocolate, vanilla, and strawberry. An ideal choice for a family or group.

parfait   A layered ice cream dessert with ice cream and syrup served in a tall, slim, cone-shaped glass, also called a parfait glass. Originally the parfait was a dessert made from egg yolks, sugar syrup, and coffee.

Philadelphia ice cream   An American-style ice cream made without a custard base (no eggs or milk) and thus somewhat grainy. Its other primary characteristic, reflecting the importance and expense that vanilla beans had in the late nineteenth century, is that it always contains visible bits of the seeds from the still-expensive vanilla bean.

plombières   Named, most likely, for the lead or "plomb" of pewter molds so popular in the late 1800s, this molded ice cream was popular in France in the nineteenth century. It was also a favorite in Italy, where it was made with candied fruit not unlike **tutti-frutti**. Although pewter molds are highly collectible, they are not always safe to use because some pewter contains high levels of lead, which does retain cold. Many manufacturers still use molds with no reports of ill effects.

Popsicle   Sherbet on a stick created by Frank Epperson, who originally called it an Epsicle. Providence and wise marketing prevailed. It contains no milk and is available in a wide range of flavors and bright colors in single or double sticks.

sa'alab   Iranian (aka Persian) ice cream that is very elastic and very white, due to its namesake ingredient, sa'alab (the ground-up root of an orchid flower). Also goes by the names of *salepi, salab,* or *salap*. Available at many Middle Eastern groceries, usually made with rosewater, saffron, or chocolate.

semi-freddo   Italian for semifrozen, this is an ice also known in Italy as a *perfetti* because it is served in a glass similar to a parfait glass. It requires no machinery or ice cream freezer and is quite a light dessert because it does not freeze as hard as a sorbet or ice cream.

sherbet   A frozen dessert made with sugar syrup, flavoring, and either 5 percent cream or milk or 1 to 2 percent butterfat. It is beaten several times during the freezing process to acquire a smooth texture. Sometimes, egg white mixed with the sugar syrup is used, but that is considered a dated technique. The difference between sherbet and **sorbet** is that sherbet does have milk or cream and sorbet usually does not have milk products, although some older techniques used cream or egg white.

sorbet   A frozen dessert made with a thick sugar syrup or sugar and flavoring. Unlike a granita, it is beaten several times during the freezing process to make the texture smooth. In the nineteenth century egg white or cream was added, but generally this is not done anymore. Some citric acid or lemon juice is added to enhance the sweetness and intensity of the fruits used. Sometimes sorbets are called "water ices" or "intermissions" and served between meals as a palate cleanser.

spoom   A lighter, more delicate sorbet made with half Italian (*spumoni*) or French meringue and half sorbet, frozen without stirring. Frequently it has fruit juice or wine and a very highly concentrated sugar syrup to make a very sweet dish. Its delicacy is in its lighter texture, a result of the meringue which is sugar and egg whites.

spumoni   An Italian dessert that is a combination of water ice and ice cream, made similar to a **bombe**. It is created in a mold with an outside layer of chocolate, vanilla, or strawberry ice cream and an inside layer of **semi-freddo** or perfetti ice of coffee, nut, or fruit.

tutti-frutti   An Italian vanilla ice cream with maraschino cherries and other similar fruit saturated in syrup; like a dundee cake or fruitcake only in ice cream.

water ice   *See* **sorbet**.

whey protein   Made by filtering fresh milk into a purified protein and used to add body and texture to ice cream. Although lactose and minerals are removed and only the protein remains, those people who are lactose-intolerant should not use anything made from whey.

yogurt   Adding friendly bacteria to milk produces yogurt, a milk that is thickened and changed in its texture. This thickening is a result of a fermentation brought on by either *Lactobacillus bulgaricus* or *Streptococcus thermophilus*. Some frozen yogurts, however, contain another friendly bacteria, *Lactobacillus acidophilus*, but others have none of these bacteria in it, or such a trace amount as to be negligible. Because of the "tangy" taste of true yogurt culture, many manufacturers add a great deal of sweeteners.

Bibliography
· ·

Chocolate, Strawberry and Vanilla: A History of American Ice Cream. Anne Cooper Funderburg, Ohio: Bowling Green State University Press, 1995.

Frozen Desserts: The Definitive Guide to Making Ice Creams, Ices, Sorbets, Gelati, and Other Frozen Delights. Caroline Liddell and Robin Weir, New York: St. Martin's Griffin, 1996. Previously published in Great Britain in hardcover by Hodder and Stoughton, 1993.

Great American Cooking Schools, Ice Cream and Ices. Nancy Arum, New York: Harper & Row, 1981.

The Great American Ice Cream Book. Paul Dickson, New York: Atheneum, 1973.

Ice Cream! Jill Neimark, New York: Hastings House Publishers, 1986.

Ice Cream, From Simple Scoops to Spectacular Desserts With Over 400 Recipes. Hillary Walden, New York: Simon and Schuster, 1985.

Ices, Plain and Fancy, The Book of Ices. A. B. Marshall, London, 1885. Reproduced by the Metropolitan Museum of Art, 1976, with annotations by Barbara Ketcham Wheaton.

Luncheonette, Ice-Cream, Beverage, and Sandwich Recipes from the Golden Age of the Soda Foundation. ed. Patricia M. Kelly, New York: Crown Publishers, Inc., 1989.

Index

Accessories, serving, 78–82
Air-inject freezer, 45
À la mode, 121
Alexander the Great, 26
Almond kulfi, 99
Anatole, Ronald and Phyllis, 117
Arabs, 25, 28
Avayou, David, 45

Baked Alaska, 40–41
Balsamic vinegar, raspberries with, 106
Bananas Foster, 120
Banana split
  basic, 117
  variations, 118
Basic banana split, 117
Basic float, 131
Basic frappé, 129
Basic frozen yogurt, 137
Basic malt, 125
Basic milk shake, 123
Basic sundae, 115
Baskin-Robbins, 50–51
Beckford, William, 141
Berry frozen yogurt, 138

Berry sorbet, 105
Birnes, William J., 55–59
Black and white sundae, 116
Blackberry shake, double rainbow Marion, 131
Black cow, 127, 133
Black currant sorbet, 106
Bladen, Thomas, 33
Books about ice cream, 15, 32, 38
Broadway, 119
  ice cream soda, 133
  soda version, 128
Brown, Cathy, 90
Brown, Craig, 140
Brown, Heywood, 122
Brown cow, 124, 134
Burt, Harry, Sr., 46
Butter pecan ice cream
  store-bought, 90

Café Procope, 15, 31–32
California kiwi sorbet, 111
Calories in frozen desserts, 139
Cantaloupe and peach yogurt, 145
Cappuccino float, 134
Caramel pear sherbet, creamy, 109

Carbohydrates in frozen desserts, 139
Carob, soybean milk and tofu ice cream with, 146
Carvel, Tom, 48
Carvel's, 91
Cassis ice cream, 98
Cathy Brown's peach ice cream, 90
Chai gelato, store-bought, 94
Champe, Sally, 75–76
Charles I, king of England, 31
China, 25
Chocolate coffee ice cream, 96
Chocolate ice cream
    basic, 87
    in Hoboken sundae, 116
    store-bought, 88
Chocolate sorbet
    soda float, Häagen-Dazs, 130
    store-bought, 88
Chocolate tofu ice cream, 145
Citrus sorbets
    about, 109
    store-bought, 111
Cleaning and cleanliness, 71, 72, 104
Cocoa choco shake, 124
Coconut deluxe sorbet, 112
Coffee, 92
Coffee extracts, 92
Coffee frozen yogurt, 138
Coffee granita, 113
Coffee ice cream
    about, 69
    chocolate, 96
    espresso, 95
    in java latté shake, 125
    store-bought, 92, 97
Coffee liqueurs, 92
Cones, 42–45
    to make, 80
Cranberry granita, 113
Cranberry ice cream, crimson, 98
Crank-type bucket freezer, 74–75
Creamy caramel pear sherbet, 109
Crimson cranberry ice cream, 98

Dairy Queen, 48–49
DeCillis, Lou, 130
De Gouy, Louis, 119
Diabetics, 143–44
Dixie Cup, 46
    lids, 54
Donvier's sugar-free ice cream, 144
Double rainbow Marion blackberry shake, 131
Doumar, Abe, 45
Drinks, ice cream, 122
    black cow, 127, 133
    Broadway soda, 128, 133
    brown cow, 124, 134
    chocolate sorbet soda float, Häagen-Dazs, 130
    float
        basic, 131
        cappuccino, 134
        chocolate sorbet soda, Häagen-Dazs, 130
        ginger beer, 135
    frappé, basic, 129
    ice cream soda
        basic, 126
        hot, 128
    malt, basic, 125
    The Manzi, 129
    milk shake
        basic, 123
        brown cow, 124, 134
    raspberry cordial smoothie, Savino, 130
    shake
        blackberry, double rainbow Marion, 131
        cocoa choco, 124
        java latté, 125
    silver slammer, 126

Earl Grey gelato, store-bought, 94
Earl Grey ice cream, 93
Electric ice cream freezers, 77
Eliot, T. S., 103
Epperson, Frank, 46
Equipment for home-made ice cream, 71–72. See also
    Ice cream machines, home
Escoffier, 120–21

Eskimo Pie, 46
Espresso, 92
Espresso gelato, store-bought, 96
Espresso ice cream, 95

Fat-free frozen desserts, 141
Fermented milk, 26
Float
    basic, 131
    cappuccino, 134
    ginger beer, 135
    Häagen-Dazs chocolate sorbet soda, 130
    root beer, largest, 65
France, 29, 31–32
Frappé, basic, 129
Freezers, home, 51. *See also* ice cream freezers
Freezer unit of refrigerator, 72–73
Frozen yogurt, 62, 63, 68, 137
    berry, 138
    cantaloupe and peach, 145
    coffee, 138
    fruit, 144
    nutritional facts, 139
Frozen yogurt, basic, 137
Fruit purées, commercial, 98
Fussell, Jacob, 38

Garlic ice cream, 100
Gelato
    chai, store-bought, 94
    Earl Grey, store-bought, 94
    espresso, store-bought, 96
    vanilla, 136
Giffy, George, 42
Ginger beer float, 135
Good Humor bar, 46
Granita
    about, 112
    coffee, 113
    cranberry, 113
Grant, Kate, 122
Grapefruit ice, 110
Green, Robert M., 42, 126

Green tea ice cream, 94
    store-bought, 95

Häagen-Dazs chocolate sorbet soda float, 130
Hamwi, Ernest A., 44, 45
Hayward, Terry, 98, 111
Henry, Marie, 82–83, 139
Henry II, King, 28–29
Hoboken sundae, 116
Hood, H. P., 46
Hot fudge, 115
Hot ice cream soda, 128
Howard Johnson restaurants and motels, 49–50

Ice
    harvesting, 36–37
    transporting, 37
Iceboxes, 37
Ice cream bar, largest, 65
"Ice Cream Concerto," 63
Ice cream desserts, 114
Ice cream freezers, 35–36
    air-inject, 45
    continuous, 46
Ice cream machines, 51, 74–77
Ice cream sandwich, largest, 65
Ice cream soda, 41–42
    basic, 126
    Broadway, 133
    hot, 128
Ice cups, 40
Ices, 25
    grapefruit, 110
Ice Screamers, The, 19, 53–55
Ingredients, 72
International Dairy Queen, 49

Java latté shake, 125
Jefferson, Thomas, 33
Johnson, Howard, 49–50
Johnson, Nancy, 35

Kabbaz, Nick, 44, 45
Keats, John, 104

Kiwi sorbet, California, 111
Kulfi, 99
   store-bought, 100
Kupferman, Meyer, 63–65

Lactose-free frozen desserts, 140–41
Lemon sherbet, 102
Liebling, A. J., 114
Lime sherbet punch, 103
Limon, Roberto, 63–65
Lincoln, Abraham, 38
Louis XIV, 30

McCullough, F. J. "Grandpa" and H. A. (Alex), 48, 49
Madison, Dolley, 35
Malt, basic, 125
Manufacturers of ice cream, 38
Manzi, Carolyn, 129
Manzi, The, 129
Marchiony, Italo, 44
Marshall, Agnes, 78
Marshall, Agnes B., 38, 40
Masser, H. B., 35–36
Masters, Thomas, 36
Medici, Catherine de, 28–29
Melba, Nellie, 120–21
Melting problems, 74
Memorabilia, 53–59
Menches, Charles, 44
Milk, fermented, 26
Milk shake
   basic, 123
   brown cow, 124
Molds, ice cream, 78–79

Nelson, Christian, 46
Nero Claudius Caesar, 27
Noble, Sherb, 48
Nutritional facts, 139

Oltz, Harry M., 49
Orange sherbet, 102

Palchak, Thomas, 141
Paper ephemera, 53–54
Parfaits, 119
Paris, 29, 31–32
Peach and cantaloupe yogurt, 145
Peaches melba, 120
Peach ice cream
   Cathy Brown's, 90
   store-bought, 91
Pear sherbet, creamy caramel, 109
Perfect Purée, The, 98
Persia, 28
Persimmon sorbet, 108
Pistachio kulfi, 100
Polo, Marco, 24–25
Popsicle, 46
Porta, Battista della, 30
Pot freezer, 77
Pre-chilled canister units, 76–77
Problems found in commercial and at-home frozen
      desserts, 73–74
Pumpkin ice cream, 144

Ranhofer, Charles, 41, 43
Raspberry cordial smoothie, Savino, 130
Raspberry sorbet, 105
   with balsamic vinegar, 106
Refrigeration, 37
Rhubarb cream, 143
Root beer, 16–17
   float. See also Black cow
      largest, 65

St. Louis World Exposition (1904), 44
Sanders, Fred, 41
Sassoon, Siegfried, 97
Savino raspberry cordial smoothie, 130
Scoop, 81–82
Servers, edible, 80. See also Cones
Serving frozen desserts, 81
Shake. See also Milk shake
   cocoa choco, 124
   java latté, 125

Sheet music, 53–54
Sherbet, 28, 31
  about, 101
  creamy caramel pear, 109
  lemon, 102
  nutritional facts, 139
  orange, 102
  punch, lime, 103
Silver slammer, 126
Smoothie, Savino raspberry cordial, 130
Soda fountain desserts, 81
Soda fountains, 54, 55–59
Soft ice cream, 48–49
Sorbet
  about, 103
  à l'americaine, 40
  berry, 105
  black currant, 106
  citrus, 109, 111
  coconut deluxe, 112
  kiwi, California, 111
  nutritional facts, 139
  persimmon, 108
  raspberry, 105
  raspberry, with balsamic vinegar, 106
  tangerine, 110
Soybean milk and tofu ice cream with carob, 146
Spade, 81–82
Sprague, Reginald, 49–50
Strawberry ice cream
  basic, 88
  store-bought, 89
Strawberry tofu ice cream, 146
Sugar-free frozen desserts, 142
  fruit yogurt, 144
Sugar-free ice cream
  Donvier's, 144
  pumpkin, 144
Sugar syrup, basic, 86
Sugar water, 104

Sundae, 41, 42
  basic, 115
  black and white, 116
  Hoboken, 116
  largest, 65
Syrup
  about, 114
  basic sugar, 86

Tangerine sorbet, 110
Tea ice cream, 92–93
  Earl Grey, 93
  green tea, 94
Teitel, Mara, 100
Texture of frozen desserts, 73–74
Thomas Jefferson's vanilla ice cream, 34
Tofu ice cream
  chocolate, 145
  soybean milk and, with carob, 146
  strawberry, 146
Tortoni, 32

Vanilla gelato, 136
Vanilla ice cream
  about, 69
  basic, 86
  store-bought, 87
  Thomas Jefferson's, 34
Villafranca, Blasius, 30
Vogt, Clarence, 46

Washington, George, 33, 77
Wemischner, Robert, 29, 107
West, Mae, 99
White Mountain Freezer, 36, 74
Williams and Company, 35
World Exposition (St. Louis, 1904), 44

Yogurt, frozen. *See* Frozen yogurt
Young, William H., 35